D0113578

EATING PROBLEMS FOR BREAKFAST

OTHER BOOKS BY TIM HANSEL

When I Relax I Feel Guilty
What Kids Need Most in a Dad
You Gotta Keep Dancin'
Holy Sweat

EATING
PROBLEMS
FOR
BREAKFAST

A Simple, Creative Approach
to Solving Any Problem

Tim Hansel

WORD PUBLISHING
Dallas · London · Sydney · Singapore

EATING PROBLEMS FOR BREAKFAST: A CREATIVE GUIDE TO PROBLEM SOLVING

Copyright 1988 by Tim Hansel

An effort has been made to locate sources and obtain permission where necessary for quotations used in this book. In the event of any unintentional omission, modifications will gladly be incorporated in future printings.

Library of Congress Cataloging-in-Publication Data
Hansel, Tim
     Eating problems for breakfast : a creative guide to problem
solving
          Bibliography: p.
          1. Conduct of life.   2. Problem solving.   I. Title.
     BJ1581.2.H27   1988   158'.1   88-37838
     ISBN 0-8499-0656-3
     ISBN 0-8499-3126-6 (pbk.)

8 9 8 0 1 2 3 9 AGF 9 8 7 6 5 4 3 2 1
Printed in the United States of America

To
Larry Johnston,
one of God's own prototypes,
a high-powered mutant who was
never even considered
for mass production
(and an exquisite problem solver)

and

my FINE* fellowship group—
Tim Gibson
Jim Weaver
Doug McGlashan
with whom I can truly be myself
and who listen to and help me wrestle
with some of my deepest
life struggles

(*We consider ourselves Fouled up, Insecure,
Neurotic, and Emotionally unstable)

Learn to eat problems for breakfast
—*Alfred Armand Montapert*

Contents

Acknowledgments

To be quite honest, even though the production of this book encouraged lots of creativity and downright fun, this has been a tough manuscript to write. My schedule for the last two years has been "somewhere to the left of whoopee!" and has not allowed me much time to write. Much of this book has been written in bits and pieces, often in the middle of the night.

Pam, Zac, and Josh have been extraordinarily patient with me tolerating all the inconveniences this book has caused, such as coming home late and kissing them good-night long after they were asleep. In the mornings, my family has had to face a cadaver-like husband and father who would prop himself up wearily at the breakfast table and mumble inarticulate quotes about problem solving that did not fit into the ongoing conversation.

But what an encouragement they have been! To help my fading spirits as the deadline drew near, Zac, my eldest son, even made me a few dozen signs and posted them all over my workroom that said "We *always rise to the occasion!*" There were times when I thought I'd never complete the project, but "We fooled 'em in the end."

Special acknowledgment and gratitude goes to Rick Vander Kam without whom this book never would have been completed. A gifted writer himself, he researched, edited, sparked ideas, and pushed his computer to the limit to complete the task. Frankly, I've never seen anyone with so much creativity and stamina on a computer! His influence is evident everywhere throughout these pages.

Dick Baltzell was more than just an editor to me. He was a cohort throughout the whole process—pushing and pulling, cheerleading and brainstorming—to make sure this project finally had wings. He was utterly indispensable to this whole production. He not only looks like Ernest Hemingway, but he thinks like him, too! His wisdom and contagious laughter will be remembered every time I pick up this book.

Jim Wilson spent many midnight hours brainstorming with me on the phone. His love for life is contagious, and many of his ideas were instrumental in the final outcome of this project. His curiosity is insatiable, and his creativity seems to know no bounds. More than once he pulled me out of a cul-de-sac of stagnation in order to keep things flowing smoothly. For those actions as well as his friendship I'm deeply grateful.

Jim Black from Word Publishing came and literally "camped" with us in our "writing studio," which is really just an old converted beauty shop. (Isn't it amazing how God can use some unusual things for His purposes?) He offered objectivity, insight, and much laughter.

Special thanks also to Chuck Maish and Candice Hay at International Graphics Engineering Systems for loaning me an extra computer at the last minute.

Jeanne Fletcher made both the typewriter and the computer keyboard dance with lightning speed during late hours after work and on weekends. Without her, we never would have met our deadline. Her unfathomable skill and cheer were both important and appreciated.

Patti Blumenthal and Anita Halstead, two of the more creative people on Planet Earth, sent invaluable articles on creativity and problem solving, for which I am grateful.

And what can I say about Erma? Those who know me, know well that I wouldn't survive without Erma Barton. She holds all the pieces together at our Summit Expedition office. She does everything—and does it well. For those of you who don't have someone as remarkable as her to work with, I can only say, "eat your heart out!"

Near the end I was almost starting to sink. I was exhausted and rather dehydrated of ideas. I was about ready to put up a white flag when Chris Slagle came to my rescue by sending me a barrage of encouragement through notes, quotes, phone calls, and friendship.

One of his cards showed Christopher Robin and all his friends (Eeyore, Tigger, and the rest of the gang) pulling Winnie the Pooh out of a tight spot. The card's inscription said: "If you're ever in a tight spot . . . you can always count on us to pull you through."

Then Chris wrote, "I just put these thoughts together to try to throw a few buckets full of water out of your boat . . . to encourage you and to remind you of the ones who really love you—your friends, your family, and your inexhaustible God."

All of these special friends and cohorts remind me of a plaque given to me some time ago. It now hangs on the old beauty shop wall amid the fragments of potpourri paperwork pieced to the walls. Amid pictures of Einstein, Mother Teresa, and Zorba the Greek, Gary Larson cartoons, and our international "No Freaking Out" sign, the plaque says:

> Once in an age, God sends to some of us, someone who loves in us, not a false imagining, or an unreal character, but looking through all of our human imperfections, loves in us the divine ideal of our nature.
>
> We call this rarest of persons, who loves us not alone with emotion, but with true understanding, a friend.

Truly I am among all men most richly blessed to have such friends.

Tim Hansel
San Dimas, California

EATING
PROBLEMS
FOR
BREAKFAST

Part 1

Until Further Notice—Celebrate Everything

Introduction:
Two Parables

Mrs. Simpson enjoyed teaching Sunday School immensely. Each Saturday she would prepare stories, lessons, and questions for her students. One Sunday morning, she asked the children, "What's gray, has a big bushy tail, has four little feet, climbs trees, and eats nuts?"

She was surprised when no hands went up and no child responded. After a brief silence, she repeated the question, "Okay, children, now picture this in your mind. What's gray, has a big bushy tail, climbs trees, eats nuts, and has four little feet."

Again, there was no response. Puzzled by the silence, she thought, "I just need to explain it a little more slowly and a little more carefully."

"Now come on children," she said. "Imagine this in your mind and see if you can give me the answer. What is gray, has a big bushy tail, has fur, has four little feet that enable it to climb trees, and eats nuts. In fact, it eats acorns . . . that's the kind of nuts it eats, acorns!"

She paused, convinced that the added clues would bring forth the correct answer. Still, there was only silence. Finally, little Johnny raised his hand timidly.

"Yes?" the teacher said. "Johnny, what's the answer?"

Johnny said, "Gee, Mrs. Simpson, it sure sounds like a squirrel, but I think I'm supposed to say, 'Jesus.'"

Moral: We can sometimes overspiritualize our problems and miss the answers.

A SECOND PARABLE

A terrible flood occurred in Mississippi one year. The great river overflowed its banks and kept rising. A nearby town was in danger, and an evacuation order was issued.

Mr. Brown was a devout Christian man who lived in the town. As the flood waters grew higher and higher and havoc raged around him, he remained calm. When the waters were as high as his porch, he rested peacefully in his hammock.

A man came by in a rowboat and said, "Mr. Brown! Mr. Brown! I'm glad I saw you. Jump in! We have to evacuate, I'll take you to safety in my rowboat."

Mr. Brown thanked the man, smiled, and said, "I'm fine. God's going to take care of me."

The flood waters continued to rise until they were approaching the windows on the second floor of Mr. Brown's house. Still, Mr. Brown remained calm. A Coast Guard boat came by, and an officer saw Mr. Brown, knee deep in water, standing near a window.

"Mr. Brown. I'm glad we saw you," the officer said. "It's getting quite dangerous, and we're one of the last rescue boats out in this weather. Jump on board and we'll take you to safety."

Mr. Brown again thanked the man, smiled, and said, "God is going to take care of me."

The flood waters continued to rise until they were almost to the top of the roof on Mr. Brown's house. By this time, Mr. Brown was sitting at the very top of his roof. The flood waters were only a few feet below him. Then, a helicopter came by and threw down a rope ladder. The pilot shouted, "Mr. Brown, I'm glad we saw you there.

This is the worst flood we've had in years. Climb up the ladder into the helicopter, and we'll take you to safety."

Mr. Brown again thanked the man, smiled, and calmly said, "God will take care of me."

The flood waters continued to rise, and Mr. Brown drowned.

When he arrived in heaven, Mr. Brown went to God and asked, "Why didn't you save me? I waited and waited, and told everybody that you were going to save me. Why didn't you do that?"

And God said, "You've got to be kidding! I sent you a rowboat, a Coast Guard boat, and a helicopter. You ignored them all!"

Moral: God gives us resources—including our minds, tools, and abilities—to solve problems, but it is our responsibility to use them.

1

For the Fun of It

To put your ideas into action is the most difficult thing in the world.

Goethe

This one is quite fundamentally different from my other symphonies. But that must be: I could never repeat a state of mind—and as life drives on, so too I follow new tracks in every work. . . . All the skill that experience has brought me is of no avail. One has to begin to learn all over again for the new thing one sets out to make. So one remains everlastingly a beginner! It is and always will be a gift of God—one that, like every loving gift, one cannot deserve and one cannot get by asking.

Gustav Mahler

In a very real sense, the writer writes in order to teach himself . . .

Alfred Kazin

7

A friend of mine sent me a card recently that sums it up pretty well. On the front of the card was a very artistic bowl of cherries. When I opened the card it said, "Life isn't."

What I have learned time and again is that to live is to have problems. So we might as well face reality together. I know of no panaceas for problems—but there *is* a hopeful process and strategy for approaching them. This book is about how to solve problems, not because I have solved all my problems but because I have so many unsolved problems on my plate, and I assume you do as well.

As I expected, I've encountered numerous problems while writing these pages. One author said that writing includes "hard work, sweat, sore limbs, bloodied fingers, callouses, aching muscles, hurting eyes, and just being tired." Believe me, I bear all the symptoms. One of the most gifted writers of our time, Chuck Swindoll, asked me recently, "Tim, is writing easy or hard for you?" I said it was hard, in fact very hard. I was relieved when he replied, "It is for me too."

I expect to get as much out of writing this book as you will reading it. Because writing about problem solving is different from anything I've wrestled with in the past, I've felt at times (as Gustav Mahler says above) like a real, true beginner. It's fun to learn all over again—taking the raw clay of experience and trying to mold it into something that is simple without being simplistic, that is creative without losing coherency, that is fun without being superficial, that is meaningful without being heavy, that is challenging without being overwhelming.

Facing this subject directly has been exhausting at times for me. For some reason, I seem to write about what I need most to learn. My first book, *When I Relax I Feel Guilty,* was aimed as much at me as at anyone else. In that book, I invited the reader to slow down, to celebrate each unpredictable day, and to savor the sacred gift of life itself. I know that the book changed at least one life—my own.

In *What Kids Need Most in a Dad,* I shared my excitement and struggles over parenting in a society which grows more complex each day. More than anything else, that book offered practical encouragement for those parents who want to be their best but sometimes can't. It forced me to rearrange some of my priorities. In my third book, *You Gotta Keep Dancin'*, I was challenged to clarify my own journey with chronic pain and to discover joy that I never knew existed in the midst of it (and I was honored when it received a national award of merit from the Evangelical Christian Publishers Association).

And *Holy Sweat* expressed my life-long fascination with the incredible and immeasurable things that God can do with a willing life.

Each book was born out of a desire to learn as well as share. Each, in its own way, clarified a major intersection in my life. Each challenged me to grow, and each continues to have that kind of impact on me. Each describes who I am struggling to become as much as who I am.

While writing this book I've had to struggle with a lot of problems. Believe me, it's a problem to put the right words together when you're up to your armpits in alligators.

I wish I could tell you that I am an expert on problem solving. But I can't. Someone once defined an expert this way: "ex = has been, and spurt is a small drip under pressure." I like that! In truth, I am an amateur in the problem-solving process, and I hope I'll always remain one! To me the word "amateur" implies the fresh excitement of continual beginnings and a passion for growth. In fact, the etymological root of "amateur" is "lover of." I believe that the ability to solve problems requires an undaunted love for life and all its varied problems.

To create is always to learn. I've learned much about the issue of problem solving as well as about myself while trying to put these pages together. My hope is that you'll learn as much by reading them, so that you'll become an amateur (a "lover of") in the process of problem solving, but more importantly that you'll learn to have fun solving your problems.

Let me encourage you though, this is not a book simply to be read. Consider it more of a workbook, a kind of living resource. Neither complex nor simplistic, this book offers no magic formulas. Instead, it describes a process, an approach, a design that you can make into your own style of problem solving. Reread, absorb, and apply these principles constantly until the process is second nature for you. It's a tool to be used, not a literary trophy that becomes another bookshelf monument.

This book belongs on your worktable or wherever your problems are. It can also be used as a source for teaching others a fun, logical, and innovative approach to problem solving. I have included various exercises which you can use in groups or alone to stretch your own creative capabilities.

One of my greatest hopes is that these pages will "put salt on your lips" to create a hunger and a thirst for more information on the subject of creative problem solving. I've included a bibliography of references at the end.

A friend from Amsterdam, Jan van den Bosch, said recently, "The tragedy in America is that most authors have a 'quick fix' formula for solving nearly everything. They've forgotten how exquisite and complex this process of life is."

He's absolutely right. Life is indeed a process. Life is a never-ending, always-changing series of continual problems. There are no typical problems. Each is unique—but we can apply a deliberate and systematic approach to solving problems that still leaves plenty of room for spontaneity and flexibility.

After deciding on the title, *Eating Problems for Breakfast*, I stumbled upon this delightful quote by Ashleigh Brilliant: "If we solve all the world's problems at breakfast, we can spend the whole day having fun!"

Problems are, or can be, the true breakfast of champions. They become the "fuel" for the future. As I'll say many times throughout this book, to live is to solve problems. Problems are the core of our existence. Therefore, problem solving is too, but few of us realize it. Problems are a central reality of existence.

What I've brought together in this book are the four major components to problem solving, including a simple, seven-step process for solving any kind of problem.

The basic premises of problem solving are:

• Problems are inevitable and unavoidable.
• They are the means by which we grow. They are not necessarily "bad."
• There is no such thing as a problem without a gift in it.

- Problem solving is one of the critical and central activities in one's life.
- Problems come in all shapes, sizes, varieties, and levels of difficulty.
- Problems grow more complex each year.
- Problem solving can be easier, more effective, and more fun if you have a flexible system for solving problems.
- There is no substitute for experience. If you want to become a better problem solver, you must practice, practice, practice. Hence, the better problem solver you become, the better problem solver you become.

Learning to "eat" problems for breakfast can be fun. These pages include a variety of problems that you can practice on and gain knowledge about which definitely transfers over into your world of difficulties.

Ultimately, the purpose of these problem-solving techniques is to take what you've learned and share God's immense love for the world by getting involved in some of the needs around you. Love will always find a way to be practical.

If you ever had a problem—or so many that you wished they would all disappear—read on. I can't guarantee that your problems will disappear, but I can help you do the next best thing: solve them. Problem solving takes work, there's no way of getting around that. But it's fun work, so you can enjoy it.

Early in the process of writing this book, I established these three immutable rules:

1. Have fun!
2. Have fun!
3. See rules one and two.

So . . .

Have fun!

2

Thank God for Problems

Peaceable people believe that faith is the solution to all problems. The fact is that faith puts all solutions into crisis. Faith is a consuming fire that reduces all certitudes into dust. To have faith means to have problems.

Abraham Heschel

In other words, *Life ain't no ride on no pink duck.*

Problems. We all know them well. They seem to be here to stay. It's been said many times, but let's say it again, "to live is to have problems." These problems come in all sizes, shapes, varieties, and styles. Some are fairly easy to solve—such as learning to tie our shoes—while many are considerably more difficult. Some problems seem to border on the impossible. I saw a card that says it well: "If you can keep your head in all this confusion, you simply don't understand the situation."

Tony Campolo was right on target when he observed in his insightful book, *Who Switched the Price Tags?* that having fun has a lot to do with living in accordance with God's priorities and with being the people God created us to be. Tony says, "Without fun, marriages don't work; when jobs aren't fun, they become intolerable and dehumanizing; when children aren't fun to be with, they are heartbreaking; when churches aren't fun, religion becomes a drag; when life is not fun, it is just plain hard." But he goes on to remind us that having fun is not a frivolous accomplishment. Instead, he says that learning to have fun is one of the most serious subjects in the world. C. S. Lewis said, "Joy is the serious business of heaven." So, while we explore the serious business of problem solving, we hope to approach it in a fun way so that you can actually take these tools and make problem solving easier and your life more fun.

Our ability to solve problems depends on our attitude, our approach, our skill, and our experience. As Chuck Swindoll said so eloquently, "We are all faced with a series of great opportunities brilliantly disguised as impossible situations."

THE INEVITABILITY OF PROBLEMS

If you have a pulse, you have problems. Whether those problems are as simple as a shoe coming apart or as complicated as a life coming apart, no one is unaffected by problems. Some problems simply aggravate us while other problems hurt us deeply for many years. Often we overcome one set of problems only to be confronted by another, more difficult set. Hence, problems are the litmus paper of the human story.

Consequently, everyone is a problem solver. Whether you are a youth worker, a lawyer, a homemaker, a student, a grocery clerk, a mechanic, a plumber, or a doctor—whatever you are—you are a problem solver. Likewise, most of us get pretty good at problem solving, but at some point we all feel a bit overwhelmed. Helen Hayes expressed it well when she said, "The toughest years in life are those between ten and seventy."

All of us encounter more problems or potential problems every day than we probably realize. If we stopped to think about it, we would also be pleased with how good we really are at solving many of those problems. Yet I have never met anyone who wouldn't like to be more competent at solving problems. Nor have I met anyone who wouldn't like to learn more about the structure and ingredients of the problem-solving process. As crucial as effective problem solving is to the fabric of our lives, it is ironic how little conscious thought is given to this subject. In all my years of schooling, I have never known of a class that was offered on the subject of creative problem solving.

In 1965, I was graduated from Stanford University with both bachelor's and master's degrees. I had studied biology, history, English, and mathematics. I had stretched my horizons with advanced classes on the educational process. I had deepened my sensitivities with classes in art and literature. I had memorized and systematized, harmonized and criticized, theorized and strategized. I had solved countless problems during my six years at Stanford. But no one—in grade school, junior high, high school, college, or graduate school—ever showed me how to solve problems. No one ever took the process apart for me, helped me to understand the basic elements of problem solving and how to put them together. I was never instructed as to what was important and what wasn't. I never knew how to approach a problem or what my attitude had to do with it all? I identified with the person who said: "If you have a college degree you can be absolutely sure of one thing . . . you have a college degree."

Why wasn't problem solving taught in school somewhere? Too often our schools have focused their teachings on *what* to think rather than on *how* to think. I doubt that anyone conspired to hide the secrets of thinking and problem solving from the general public. Instead, like many of us, most educators solve problems intuitively; thus, they are not conscious of their own basic processes of problem solving. It just doesn't occur to them to teach problem solving as a learnable skill.

Few people have a strategy for solving problems. In twenty years of teaching, I have found only a handful of students, and even teachers, who have a clear, concise method for approaching problems. When problems arise at inconvenient times, most of us react rather than respond. Many times, the solutions we react with work, at least temporarily. So, most of us don't take the time to find better, longer-lasting solutions. Unfortunately, as problems become more complex, the solutions that come from this reaction method commonly create more problems than they solve. When this happens and we again react rather than respond, our problems multiply with increasing momentum and sometimes with results that are tragic. If we learn genuine problem-solving techniques, we can avoid this complication of "react first and react again."

NEW PROBLEMS SURROUND US TODAY

Many problems today are new. They are not the same as they were even five years ago. If life's problems seem more frustrating, consider for a moment what you are up against. Our entire economic system is undergoing an upheaval of unprecedented proportions. Many people must make career changes and retrain themselves to meet the demands of a changing economy. In many areas of the country, mortgages have skyrocketed, placing increasing pressures on the already-overburdened family unit. In turn, this at times has led to a spiraling number of single-parent families. Even for two-parent families, economic survival often requires that both parents find work outside the home, leaving the crucial task of training our next generation in the hands of preschool facilities and television executives. Many parents are exhausted from the grind and the upheaval, and their children resort to disruptive behavior in an attempt to gain the attention their exhausted fathers and mothers are unable to give them. Clearly, if you are feeling frustrated and pressured these days, you have good reason.

From all available indicators, our society is not coping well with the current pressures on individuals, families, and institutions. We are increasingly defensive and must struggle just to hold our ground.

Nowhere is this more apparent than among our young. John Q. Baucom, in his book *Fatal Choice*, reports, "Today, teenagers face a monumental amount of change and an unhealthy abundance of information. . . . In many cases, teenagers literally live in a state of shock. The unbelievable kinds of changes and the tempo of their occurrence is simply more than they can cope with."

The result is that nearly two million teenagers will attempt to take their own lives, and some six thousand will succeed, all in the coming year. At Summit Expedition I see more and more kids stressed to a breaking point. When asked at the end of a twenty-one-day course what he had gained, one young man said, "I've learned that it's OK to fail. I don't have to be perfect at everything. Everybody has all these high expectations of me. I was feeling as if I couldn't hold it together much longer. . . . So I was thinking about killing myself, but now I don't want to do that any more." Problems that were once "just part of growing up" today carry a frightening potential for an adolescent.

Even for adults, the old problems seem to carry a much bigger impact, and the new ones present themselves with increasing frequency. Besides the more publicized methods of escape, such as suicide and drug and alcohol abuse, many teenagers and adults are hiding behind the masks of self-reliance and never-a-problem religion.

THE PURPOSE OF PROBLEMS

It has been said that there is no such thing as a problem that didn't have a gift in it.

In his wonderful book *If God Cares, Why Do I Still Have Problems?* Lloyd Ogilvie says, "The greatest problem we all share, to a greater or lesser degree, is a profound misunderstanding of the positive purpose of problems. Until we grapple with this gigantic problem, we will be helpless victims of our problems all through our lives."

Ingrained in our thinking are three false ideas about problems. It is these which I believe cause us to miss the creative purpose of problems.

False Idea Number 1: We believe that there is something inherently bad about problems because they often involve us in unpleasant pressures, distressing conflict, or an inconvenient interruption of our plans for a smooth and easy life.

False Idea Number 2: We think that lack of problems should be a reward for hard work, careful planning, and clear thinking. Present within each of us is the hope that eventually—out ahead somewhere, sometime—our life will be free of problems of any kind.

False Idea Number 3: We think that if we love God, commit our lives to Him and diligently serve Him, He will work things out for us so that everything will run smoothly for us and we will be free from problems. When it doesn't work that way we ask why is this or that happening to us. We find it easy to believe that unbelievers or scoundrels have problems but inevitably we ask why does a just and loving God permit us to experience difficulties and hard times. We are always ready to accept and praise Him for our blessings, but we fail to see that so often our problems are really blessings in disguise.

Most people think of problems as something bad, as some terrible interruption in their lives which they wish they did not have to endure. In truth, problems in and of themselves are not necessarily bad. It is interesting to note the actual Greek root of the word "problem," namely, *probalein*, means to throw, to drive, or to thrust forward. Problems are the very means by which God changes us, transforms us, and drives us forward. Without problems, there would be no growth.

Thomas Merton, one of the great spiritual writers of our century, said: "A life without problems is hopeless." It is vital to realize that problems are not only inevitable but also important for us. They play a far more significant role in our lives, in our growth, than we would ever imagine.

Since problems are with us always, there is a clear need for a well thought-out approach to solving problems. While no system of problem solving can relieve all the pressures we face, a competency in creative problem solving can help us organize our existing resources so that problems become a source of strength rather than weakness. While many would claim that we are moving into age of unprecedented difficulty, I would contend that we are also moving into an age of unprecedented opportunity.

While many, if not most, of us wish at least on some days that our problems would all go away, few of us realize how much we would lose in the process. Without problems there would be no learning, no growth, no opportunity to change. Robert Weider said, "Obstacles are your friends; you can't grow without them." A life without problems is a life without meaning. Relationships would inevitably be shallow, our films would lose their plots, our jobs would lose their purposes. Such a problem-free existence would empty books of most of their pages. Most industries would have to shut down. Inevitably we would be left with a barren existence.

I asked a good friend what he thought life would be like without problems. After a few moment's reflection, he said, "I think a person who has no problems is in serious trouble. I know that might sound strange, but if you think about it, it's our problems that provide us with growth opportunities. In all probability, a lot of businesses would go bankrupt because most of them exist to solve problems. A family without problems is really kidding itself. Relationships within that family would lack depth and probably wouldn't survive, and the children could not possibly mature into adults without the opportunity to solve many problems."

Perhaps like me, you have a tendency to want to protect your children from having problems. Yet on a deeper level we must hope that they encounter many significant problems in their lives, so that they can become mature people of God.

Perhaps this is why the writer of the Book of James says in essence, "Consider yourself blessed when you have lots of problems. In fact, rejoice and be overjoyed when you are enveloped in difficulties, trials, and hardships—for you know that these will serve to develop your faith, your endurance, and your steadfastness. In fact, if you hang in there with those problems, you will become competent and fully developed—lacking in nothing."

Problems are not only inevitable, they are a critical part of our growth. They mean you are alive and well. If you are healthy and involved in life and celebrating it to the fullest, then you've got your share of problems.

Even if I could take away all your problems, I wouldn't want to. What I hope to do is this:

1. Give you a different perspective on your problems,
2. Enable you to see them more clearly, and
3. Help you work on them more effectively.

Let me invite you to try something quite daring and bold: try celebrating your problems! In the process, you might just learn how to enjoy your problems, one of the first steps to growing through them. Often, the more difficult the problem, the more rewarding the solution.

Such an approach needs to be genuine. Most of us are like ducks swimming in a pond: we look composed on the surface but underneath the water we're paddling like crazy. Problem solving is not simply learning to cope with problems, or toughening up to endure them. Problem solving is a proactive attitude toward problems, a systematic response to a problem.

PROFOUND SIMPLICITY

> The laws of physics should be simple. . . . [if they were not] I would not be interested in them.
>
> *Albert Einstein*

In his book, *Profound Simplicity*, Will Schutz describes three progressive levels of thinking. The first stage, *simplistic*, is an immature process that usually lacks or ignores difficult but vital information. This kind of thinker addresses only the superficial elements of problems. They accept and speak in cliches because they have not thought reflectively: the world is black and white, cause results in effect (for example, "If I don't do this, then . . ."). Simplistic thinkers will say:

If you just turn the problem over to God, He will solve it.

If you only believed more, you wouldn't be having these problems.

These problems must be because you have some sin in your life.

If you only went to church more, you wouldn't be having these problems.

If only you'd tithed . . .

The second stage of thinking is what Schutz calls *complexity*. These thinkers often gather so many conflicting details that they cannot organize it into one encompassing statement. By failing to pick out significant information, this thinker is often sidetracked by details. Have you ever asked somebody a simple question only to get a thirty-minute lecture that deals with the ontological basis of life and a review of the sociological history of the world? Sometimes these answers include endless recitals from the most recent book the person has read or a multitude of Bible verses, some of which have nothing to do with the questions you asked, or explanations that include the ramifications of most of your childhood thoughts.

> According to the Benet Gestalt theory of the sociological phe-
> nomenon of the historical interaction between people in this
> sort of a relational setting, we can discover that the etymolog-
> ical root of your situation belongs to a category of words . . .
>
> Yes, I did go to Harvard, and I do remember dealing with a
> case that was very similar to yours in one of my psychology
> classes . . .
>
> Now if you could just explain to me what your feelings were at
> the age of four . . .
>
> I remember having a class on hermeneutics in seminary
> that dealt with the existential reality of situations such as
> yours . . .

The third way of thinking is what Schutz called *profound simplicity*. In this phase, thinkers have pondered the problem or subject long and deep enough to know what is truly essential. They have discarded interesting, though extraneous data to allow the gravity of truth to become apparent (which is neither simplistic nor overly complex). This is the finest, most mature kind of thinking. It is essentially what we have often called "wisdom," which comes after years of experience.

Both simplistic and overly complex thinking can be ways of evading significant issues. While the simplistic focuses on avoiding what you don't know, the complex focuses proudly on what you do know. The "profoundly simple" emphasizes the person and the situation in the clearest way and attempts to discover what is really needed for a solution.

For example, Karl Barth, a famous theologian and author of more than sixty volumes of theology, was once asked by a reporter, "Sir, what is the most profound thought you've ever had?" The young reporter realized that this was a somewhat ridiculous

question to ask a man of such knowledge and renown. Nevertheless, the theologian, seeing this realization dawn on the reporter,
said, "Yes, I do have a reply. I can respond to your question. 'Jesus
loves me, this I know, for the Bible tells me so.'"

Near the end of his life. Robert Frost, the poet, was asked a
similar question. Frost said, "Life goes on."

I didn't think these anecdotes were profound when I first read of
them while in college. Amazingly, the longer I live, the more profound they seem to me.

I have read countless approaches to problem solving over the
past twenty years. In my attempts to isolate the profoundly simple
components of creative problem solving I have come up with four
major components:

1. Attitude
2. Principles
3. Process
4. Experience

They could be diagrammed as follows:

In the following chapters we will explore each of these components in more detail.

3

Attitude:
The Critical Difference

With the right attitude, all the problems in the world will not make you a failure. With the wrong mental attitude, all the help in the world will not make you a success.

Warren Deaton

He was the sort of man who would go after Moby Dick with a row boat, a harpoon, and a jar of tartar sauce.

The first and perhaps most important component of the problem-solving process is attitude. Your attitude is the key. It is the absolute core in your effort to solve problems. I cannot overestimate how important it is. Some experts believe that 90 percent of all problem solving revolves around one's attitude. By definition, *attitude* refers to:

1. one's mental posture toward a problem or a situation;
2. one's feelings or emotions toward the problem;
3. the angle or positions of one's frame of reference.

It's not so much what happens to us, as what happens *in* us that counts, or what we *think* has happened to us.

Consider the following illustration. I overheard some golfers talking not too long ago, and one was saying, "What an incredible course this is. It has a wicked dog leg. It has two huge sand traps. There is a pond on the left." He went on describing all the obstacles on the course, and then he said, "I *love* it! It's the most exciting course I've ever played!!" Yes, he said, "I *love* it!" And he did. He loved it because it was difficult, and it brought out his best golfing skills.

This golfer had the right attitude about the course, and consequently he turned something difficult into something fun and stimulating.

Life is a process: a complex ever-continuing, ever-changing set of problems. The choice is not if you'll accept problems, but *How!* Your attitude determines whether or not you will succeed. William James said, "Perhaps the greatest discovery of this century is that if you can change your attitude, you can change your life."

Bruce Bowman agrees, saying, "The mind can convince a competent person that he is incompetent or an adequate person that he is highly talented. Unfortunately self-doubt and negative attitudes seem to have a more powerful influence on the mind than positive attitudes. Usually a person is not even aware that he is setting himself up or limiting his capabilities."[1]

---

[1] Bruce Bowman, *Ideas: How to Get Them* (Saratoga, Calif.: R&E Publishers, 1985), 21.

ARE YOU A GOOD PROBLEM SOLVER?

Your answer to the question "Are you a good problem solver?" is more important than you may think. Many, if not most, will say "no" or "probably not." I don't blame anyone who says that. I've said that myself for much of my life. When I ask that question in problem-solving seminars, normally less than 5–10 percent respond affirmatively. I try to remind these people that each of them has solved thousands of problems in their life journey thus far; so, although they all can improve, most are pretty good at solving problems already.

The tragedy is that if you think you are a poor problem solver, you probably are. Henry Ford once said, "Those who say they can and those that say they can't are usually both right."

In *A Whack on the Side of the Head*, Roger Von Oeck tells a story about attitude and creativity. He said that an oil company, hoping to stimulate its research and development people, hired psychologists to determine the characteristics of creative people. These psychologists asked the company's scientists about their education and family backgrounds, as well as their personal preferences (like favorite colors and so forth). After a three-month study, a single factor was found that determined how creative a person is—attitude. Creative people believed that they were creative; those who weren't creative didn't believe that they were.

Those people who believe themselves to be poor problem solvers usually end up fulfilling their own prophecy. Likewise, those who believe themselves to be good, creative problem solvers are confident in their skills and willing to take on all types of problems. If they fail, they realize that this is just another part of life's educational process, another opportunity to grow and gain experience.

When I was twenty-seven, a friend approached me and asked me if I was a good problem solver. I responded, "Definitely not! In fact, I am very poor at problem solving." Fortunately, he pursued the question rather than just letting it go. "You have a master's degree from one of the finest institutions in the country. You seem to have a bright and creative mind. You appear to be very capable and competent in most situations. Why aren't you a good problem solver?"

I didn't have a good answer for him. "I don't know," I said, "I just always considered myself a lousy problem solver." Quietly but firmly he reminded me, "You can be as great at problem solving as you want to be."

That conversation was a real turning point for me. From that moment on, I decided to approach problems with a totally different attitude. These days, when problems begin to overwhelm me, I remind myself that I love challenges and that these apparent obstacles are the very process by which I can become all of who I want to be.

LET THE EXPERT DO IT

Many of our attitudes about problem solving come from our upbringing. My family was steeped in the Norwegian tradition. Each holiday, especially Christmas, our home was adorned with krumkake, fattigman, lefsa, hjortetak, spritz, and all the Norwegian delicacies. My parents were second-generation Norwegians, spoke Norwegian fluently, and were proud of their rich heritage. They were also deeply proud that we were Americans.

When I was young, I wanted to help out in certain situations where my father thought I shouldn't. For example, when we went to the gas station, I wanted to pump the gasoline, but Dad would say, "Let the expert do it." It didn't seem all that difficult as I watched, but I soon developed the attitude that I was incapable of doing such functions. If the faucet dripped, my natural curiosity led me to figure out how to fix it. Then I would hear my father say, "Let the expert do it." If we had electrical problems, he would call for the "expert." If there was a need in any area, my father always turned to these "experts." Now, my parents were very good, hard-working people (and solved countless problems in their work), but Dad considered anything involving a speciality outside his area of expertise untouchable. "Let the expert do it," he said.

I soon adopted my dad's approach. Little by little the cycle was reinforced, and the process trained me to see myself as a poor problem solver. I was never told that I was a poor problem solver. In fact, I was encouraged to do well in my school work. I was praised when I did a good job. With anything that was deemed as a "problem," however, I felt that somewhere out there was an "expert" who could do it better than I could. Hence, I grew up avoiding "problems" or anything outside of my limited awareness."

This cycle continued for years and would have gone on much longer had it not been for someone intervening and instructing me that I could be as good a problem solver as I wanted to be. All I needed to do was simply apply myself and learn some basic principles.

If I accomplish nothing more in this book, I hope I can open your eyes to the possibility of your changing your attitude and becoming a good creative problem solver. Once you say "yes, I can" (and really believe it), you'll be amazed at how much your problem-solving abilities will improve automatically.

The first, key step—perhaps the most critical step in problem solving—is to learn how to meet problems head on. Lean into them, face them squarely, and attack them creatively. You must learn to "eat problems for breakfast." Your choice of attitude is the single most important ingredient affecting your abilities as a problem solver, and you are the only one who has that choice. Your attitude must be one of boldness.

The Bible says in Philippians 2 that we can have the mind of Christ. Jesus never ran away from anything, anybody, or any problem. God doesn't ask us *if* we will accept the inevitable problems of life. They are a reality. The only question we have to address is *how* we confront our problems.

The words "attitude" and "aptitude" (defined as "one's ability to solve problems effectively") both derive from the Latin word for "fitness." Our attitudes are the driving force behind our aptitude, our capacity for learning, and for solving problems. Hence, the first obstacle we must overcome is the sticky problem of assuming we can't do anything.

A faulty attitude not only constricts our ability to solve problems, but it can also cause us to look incorrectly at a problem and distort our understanding of it. Having a clear, strong attitude gives you the ability to see problems from all angles and will enhance your problem-solving abilities tremendously.

One of the most liberating discoveries of my life was that problems have positive and redemptive purposes: they can be potential blessings. They can be a means for growth. As a Christian, I also know that in Christ I have the capacity to be a very capable problem solver.

The Bible encourages us to have a sane estimate of our abilities, to be honest about ourselves. Many people interpret this to mean that we should think less of ourselves. I believe that our greatest problem is our self-limitation. In having a more sane estimate of our abilities, we need to realize the incredible things that God can do in us and through us. When we do that, we become much less intimidated by problems because we know that God is not only for us but in us. Therefore, I am not afraid to fail.

What's your attitude about life? What's your attitude about problems? What's your attitude about other people? Perhaps most important of all, what's your attitude about yourself? Are you able to see yourself as God sees you? Until we can see ourselves as God sees us, we can never accept ourselves unconditionally. How we feel about ourselves reflects our attitudes in all the other areas of our life, too.

The Bible tells us not to judge one another. By this, I think God intends for us not to judge ourselves either. Paul tells us there is no condemnation for those who live in Christ.

My wife taught me something important on this subject. One evening she said, "You know I think that great passage on love in 1 Corinthians 13 is a pattern for how we're suppose to love ourselves as well as other people." She suggested that if we read that passage each day for a few months and applied that kind of love to ourselves, our lives would be transformed dramatically. We're called to love ourselves with a love that is patient and kind, not envious or rude, that does not even demand its own way and is not irritable or touchy. It does not hold grudges. Love is quick to forgive. Those passages say when we love someone, we will always expect the best of them and will always stand our ground protecting them. Think about that! God really does love us like this.

Therefore, let us love ourselves as God loves us. When we do, we will see the amazing changes such an attitude will bring into our lives. When we see ourselves and our problems through God's eyes, we become willing to let go of our puny images and preconceptions. "What we see" is a product of what we believe we are seeing. As someone said so beautifully, "we see things not as they are, but *as we are.*" Our fitness for problem solving has much to do with a full acceptance of ourselves and our situation. The more fully we let God love us and use us, the more we will be able to celebrate those problems that are a part of the fabric of our lives.

ARE YOU A PESSIMIST OR AN OPTIMIST?

An optimist may see a light where there is none, but why must the pessimist always run to blow it out?

Michel de Saint-Pierre

I have heard it said that a person's life is based on what his thoughts are, what his basic attitude is about life. A pessimist sees a problem in every opportunity whereas an optimist sees an opportunity in every problem.

John Haggai, in his fine book *How to Win over Worry*, relates the following classic story of the difference between the two attitudes:

There were two farmers. One was a pessimist and the other was an optimist. When the sun was shining, the optimist would say, "Wonderful sunshine," but the pessimist would respond, "Yeah, but I'm afraid it's going to scorch the crops." When it rained, the optimist would say, "Fine rain," but the pessimist would respond, "Yeah, but I'm afraid we're going to have a flood."

One day the optimist said to the pessimist, "Have you seen my new bird dog? He's the finest money can buy." The pessimist said, "You mean that little mutt I saw penned up behind your house? He don't look like much to me." The optimist said, "Well, how about going hunting with me tomorrow?" The pessimist agreed.

They went and shot some ducks. The ducks landed in the pond. The optimist ordered his dog to go get the ducks. The dog obediently responded, but instead of swimming in the water, the dog walked on top of the water, retrieved the ducks, and then walked back on top of the water. The optimist now turned confidently to his pessimist friend hoping that this would have impressed him. The determined pessimist replied, "hmm . . . can't swim, can he?"

Attitude is everything. I phoned a special friend of mine, Jack Meyer, a developer, during what was probably the most difficult time of his life. "How're you doing, Jack?" His response surprised me. "Terrific! In fact, unbelievable!" I was so caught off guard by his response that I hardly knew what to say. "Jack, has the market gone up?" (It was my understanding that this was the toughest time possible in his business.) "Has there been a significant change in your situation?" "No," Jack said. "It's just that I realized what a phenomenal opportunity I have to learn. I probably have the privilege of learning more right now because of all these opportunities disguised as problems than at any other time in my life. It's really a privilege isn't it, Tim?"

When I hung up the phone, I realized again how distinctly important one's attitude is and how critical it is that we orient ourselves properly to our problems.

As Eugene Kennedy said, "One of the most common and naive sentences in the English language is perhaps the following: 'If I can just get through this problem, then everything will be all right.' There comes a time—and it may well be the birth of maturity—when we come to realize that when we get through our present problems, there will probably be another one, perhaps slightly more difficult, waiting to take its place."

Most of the psalms were born in difficulty. Most of the epistles were written in prison. The critical difference in what is accomplished is attitude. It's never too late to begin to become a competent problem solver.

Scott Peck became nationally known through his bestselling book *The Road Less Traveled*. In it, he shares a personal experience that dramatically changed his journey toward becoming a better problem solver:

When he was thirty-seven, he didn't know how to fix things. All his attempts at minor repairs somehow went wrong. Eventually he decided that, despite having a medical degree and a thriving psychiatric practice, he was a mechanical "idiot."

One day he came across a neighbor repairing his lawn mower. Peck praised him for his ability, only to be told that "anybody" could do, it just takes a little time. Peck thought about his neighbor's attitude and decided that next time he faced a minor repair he would go about solving it slowly.

Some time later the parking brake stuck on a patient's car. Coming to her aid, he crawled under the car's dashboard to find something that would release the brake. He paused for a moment and reminded himself to take his time and go slowly. Despite the maze of colored wires and gobs of tubing he eventually traced the path of the brake wires. He realized that a small latch was preventing the brake's release and that he should press upward on the latch with his finger. The problem was solved—as well as a little self-esteem.

We, too, can master new skills by changing our attitudes about them. Perhaps we need to remember constantly the motto that hung on the wall of a research department: "This problem, when solved, will be simple."

REASONS FOR SAYING "I CAN'T"

As Scott Peck discovered, perhaps the main reason for saying "I can't" is the false assumption that we are not good problem solvers and can't learn to be one. Preconceived notions make us think a problem is too difficult for us. Oddly enough, when that is our assumption, we make it come true.

The second reason for saying "I can't" is that we magnify our problems instead of our Lord. We humans have the capacity to distort almost anything. Consider the following paraphrased portion of a well-known verse in Psalm 34 (the Hansel version): "O come let us magnify our problems together. Let us talk about them until they become impossible." We magnify our problems by doubt, anxiety, worry, procrastination, and self-preoccupation. How many times have you heard someone say, "My problems are worse than anyone else's."

Instead, consider the following possibilities: try sharing the problem as accurately as possible with a friend. Through your communication with each other, try to get a properly proportioned approach to the problem. It's good to start by remembering that "problem" comes from the Greek word that means "to drive or to thrust forward." Think through questions like: Can this problem benefit me in any way? What are its assets? What are its possibilities? What are some different angles or attitudes for looking at this problem? How can I restate this problem in such a way that it will work for me?

You may have heard the famous story of the shoe salesman who was sent to Africa into a territory unreached by this particular shoe company. The eager salesman got on the plane and aggressively went about his work of trying to sell shoes. Three weeks later, however, he phoned the president, very frustrated, and said, "Send me a plane ticket, I'm coming back. Didn't you realize that people over here don't wear shoes? This job is impossible."

The company sent him a return ticket but some months later hired a woman who was excited about the possibilities. She got to Africa and three weeks later phoned the company's president. He was anticipating the same kind of response from her but was surprised to hear her say, "This place is amazing, the possibilities are endless. What an incredible opportunity! Do you realize that the people over here don't have shoes? This job is wonderful!"

It all depends on how you look at it, doesn't it?

The third reason for saying "I can't" is lack of encouragement and perhaps a lack of gratitude. Have you ever spent time with someone who could give you ninety-three reasons why a problem can't be solved? Have you ever been around someone who has all sorts of elaborate methods for justifying why the situation is impossible?

I suppose that bumping into people like this is somewhat inevitable, but I would strongly recommend you not spend a majority of your time with them, especially when you are dealing with significant problems. Spend time with people who are supportive, who are hopeful, who give you encouragement, excitement, and hope about your predicament.

Lack of encouragement and ingratitude seem to go together. People who are truly thankful for life will usually be supportive and encouraging. The word "encouragement" means "to put courage into," and since life is often so notoriously difficult, we need all the encouragement that we can get. Jean Houston, a brilliant author and speaker, says, "Perhaps encouragement is the greatest and single most powerful gift that God has ever given us. Nothing seems to impact our lives as much as encouragement."

Finally, one of the most common reasons why we say "I can't" results from our fear of failure. Ironically, our most important learning experiences often result from failure. "One of the reasons why mature people stop growing and learning," says John Gardner, "is that they become less and less willing to risk failure."

Most of what we call wisdom and experience is based on learning from our failures. Faith, it is said, makes life possible—it does not make it easy. Most successes are built on a foundation of many failures. If you are to grow as a problem solver, you must learn to "fail successfully."

REASONS FOR SAYING "I CAN"

Perhaps the best reason for saying I can is the fact that we serve a living God who enables us to do all things through Christ who lives within us. The Bible is basically a book about problems—lots of problems—and how God enabled men and women to solve them. The basic "attitude" of Scripture is that our problems are normal and vital and that God can help us solve them. Our current problems are probably not a surprise to God. They may break His heart, as they sometimes break ours, but they don't surprise Him. As someone once said, "God never has to say 'Oops!'"

Will Durant, the great historian, said, "When people ask me to compare the twentieth century to older civilizations, I always say the same thing: 'The situation is normal.'"

"We live in the midst of alarms; anxiety clouds the future; we expect some new disaster with each newspaper we read." That statement sounds current, but it was reported in a newspaper more than a hundred years ago. Its author? Abraham Lincoln.

The point of this: we cannot afford to sit back and let problems "solve themselves." We must be better problem solvers than those before us. In all of this, we must remember that God isn't wringing His hands wondering what to do next.

The Bible assumes that we are going to have problems. Isaiah didn't say, "If you go through problems." He said "When you go through problems, God will be there with you." The Bible tells by example after example that God allows us to encounter numerous problems—big, small, medium, long term, short term, or whatever—in order to help us discover a new fullness of life in Him. Problems are "the most practical way to find the power of His indwelling life."[2]

Peter's second epistle states that we can actually participate in God's divine nature (2 Pet. 1:4). If we are privileged to have this remarkable identity with the living God, then why shouldn't we be able to solve some of our problems through the resources of who He is? Being a Christian in no way guarantees that life will be easier or more "successful." Being a Christian simply guarantees each of us an inseparable link with the absolute Resource that can empower us in any circumstance.

So, when facing a problem, you need to ask yourself these three questions:

1. What is your attitude toward the problem?
2. Who is in control of the problem? Who is really responsible for it?
3. Where is the Lord in relationship to the problem? As Norman Wakefield points out, our problems are given to us deliberately to make us turn to our Father and discover the truth of all that the Scriptures teach about Him.[3]

A. W. Tozer once remarked, "The man who comes to a right belief about God is relieved of ten thousand temporal problems for he sees at once that these have to do with matters which at the most cannot concern him very long."

Wakefield tells the story of the famous inventor Samuel Morse who was once asked if he ever encountered situations where he didn't know what to do. Morse responded, "More than once, and

---

[2] Norman Wakefield, *Solving Problems Before They Become Conflicts* (Grand Rapids, Mich.: Zondervan Publishing House, 1987), 38.
[3] Ibid., 39, 41.

whenever I could not see my way clearly, I knelt down and prayed
to God for light and understanding."

Morse received many honors from his invention of the tele-
graph but felt undeserving: "I have made a valuable application of
electricity not because I was superior to other men but solely because God, who meant it for mankind, must reveal it to someone
and He was pleased to reveal it to me."[4]

WHAT SHOULD BE MY ATTITUDE
TOWARD PROBLEMS?

Remember the words of James: "Consider it pure joy, my brothers, whenever you face trials of many kinds, because you know
that the testing of your faith develops perseverance. Perseverance
must finish its work so that you may be mature and complete, not
lacking anything" (James 1:2–4, NIV).

A person who uses problems positively, as opportunities to
grow, will benefit greatly from them. Viewed in this way, problems
become a source of joy.

In his *Interpretation of Hebrews and James*, R. C. Lenski says,
"When trials come, a lot of joy comes to people of faith. There is
no denial that trials also produce strain and pain; there is, however,
a reminder that when they come and we evaluate them aright, we
ought to bear them with joy. The flesh will not like them, but the
spirit will rejoice to prove itself and to gain from the trial what
Christ intended should be gained for us."

FOR THOSE WHO STRUGGLE WITH ATTITUDE

Perhaps you are like me and struggle to keep an appropriate
attitude toward problems. One recommendation is to read books
on problem solving, motivation, and attitude. Although I have
read countless books on these subjects in the last twenty years,
one book was the most helpful. It far outweighs any other book I
have ever read on the subject. It not only has better ideas to
suggest but actually offers facts to help you with your attitude.

---

[4] Ibid., 89.

You can find this book in most bookstores. In fact you can find it in most homes. It's been a bestseller for centuries—the problem is that many of us simply don't read it. It's been called "The Book." It's a guaranteed attitude changer. In fact, it's a guaranteed life changer. It's the Bible. I highly recommend it.

Someone said of the Bible:

Know it—in your head;
Stow it—in your heart;
Sow it—in the world;
Show it—in your life.

William Lyon Phelps said, "A knowledge of the Bible without a college degree is far more valuable than a college degree without the knowledge of the Bible." Many books have been written to provide information, but the Bible was written to create transformation.

PROBLEMS ARE NORMAL AND BIBLICAL

The Bible clearly teaches that to have faith is to have problems. This contradicts those who today preach a "health and wealth gospel" implying that the more faith we have the less problems we will have. Actually the opposite is true. Daniel's faith may have gotten him out of the lion's den, but don't forget his faith got him *into* the lion's den as well. From the first book until the last, the Bible is filled with examples of how God helped people solve problems.

People in both the Old and New Testaments struggled with problems. Abraham must have struggled immensely with the thought of having to sacrifice his own son. Moses struggled for forty years to lead a group of rebellious, ungrateful people through the desert. David's life was one problem after another. Poor Elijah almost got overwhelmed by his many problems.

The Apostle Paul is sometimes referred to as the greatest Christian who ever lived, but look at what he encountered:

He received the thirty-nine-lashes penalty five times.
He was beaten three times with rods.
He was stoned.
He was shipwrecked three times.

In his own words, he said, "In my travels I have been in constant danger from rivers, from bandits, from my own countrymen, and from pagans. I have faced danger in city streets, danger in the desert, danger on the high seas, danger among false Christians. I have known drudgery, exhaustion, many sleepless nights, hunger and thirst, fasting, cold and exposure." Then he said, "Apart from all external trials I have the daily burden of responsibility for all the churches" (2 Cor. 11:26–28, PHILLIPS).

In addition to all that, Paul had a physical handicap, a "thorn in the flesh." He begged the Lord three times to take it away, but when it persisted, Paul concluded that it kept him humble and enabled him to grow spiritually (2 Cor. 12:7–10).

All this occurred after he became a Christian. Should we expect anything more, or anything better? Nevertheless, Paul's writings indicate he tried to see the creative side of his stress and used his problems as growing experiences for himself and others.

Many Christians feel pressed on every side by troubles, but we know we are not crushed and broken by them. We are often perplexed because we don't know why things happen as they do, but we don't give up and quit. We are hunted down, but God never abandons us. We get knocked down, but we get up again and keep going.

Our bodies constantly face death, just as Jesus did; so it is clear to all that it is only the living Christ within us who keeps us safe (2 Cor. 4:8ff.).

Yes, we live with constant problems because we serve the Lord, but we gain repeated opportunities to show the power of Jesus Christ in our lives.

The Bible is an amazing book. Job had more than his share of problems, yet he says, "Though He slay me, yet I will trust Him" (Job 13:15, NKJV).

Psalm 37 says, "Fret not yourself because of the wicked, be not envious of wrongdoers! For they will soon fade like the grass and wither like the green herb. Trust in the Lord, and do good; so you will dwell in the land, and enjoy security. Take delight in the Lord, and he will give you the desires of your heart. Commit your way to the Lord; trust in him, and he will act. . . . Be still before the Lord, and wait patiently for him" (Ps. 37:1–5, 7, RSV).

This passage indicates some of the critical ingredients of attitude:

1. Do not worry.
2. Trust in the Lord.
3. Take delight in Him.
4. Commit your way to the Lord.
5. Finally, be still, rest in Him, and wait patiently.

We are told on countless occasions in the Bible that if we pray and ask for God's wisdom, He will give it to us in abundance. For example, God said to Daniel, "I have now come to give you insight and understanding" (Dan. 9:22, NIV). In James it says so clearly, "If, in the process, any of you does not know how to meet any particular problem he has only to ask God—who gives generously to all" (James 1:5, PHILLIPS*). Then, he continues, "If any of you lacks wisdom, he should ask God, who gives generously to all without finding fault, and it will be given to him. But when he asks, he must believe and not doubt, because he who doubts is like a wave of the sea, blown and tossed by the wind. That man should not think he will receive anything from the Lord; he is a *double-minded* man, unstable in all he does" (James 1:5–8, NIV).

The word "worry" actually means "to divide the mind." Paul says, "Don't worry over anything whatever; whenever you pray tell God *every detail* of your needs in thankful prayer, and the peace of God, which surpasses human understanding, will keep constant guard over your hearts and minds as they *rest* in Christ Jesus" (Phil. 4:6, PHILLIPS, emphasis added).

Note again that Jesus says we will have troubles (John 16:33) but then encourages us to be of good cheer. He says let not your hearts be troubled (John 14:1). Jesus boldly encourages us to be "anxious in nothing." In one of the most beautiful passages of the New Testament He says:

don't worry about living—wondering what you are going to eat or drink, or what you are going to wear. Surely life is more important than food, and the body more important than the clothes you wear. Look at the birds in the sky. They never sow nor reap nor store away in barns, and yet your Heavenly Father feeds them. Aren't you much more valuable to him than they are? *Can any of you, however much he worries, make himself even a few inches taller?* And why do you worry about clothes? Consider how the wild flowers grow. They neither work nor weave, but I tell you that even Solomon in all his glory was not arrayed like one of these! Now if God so clothes the flowers of the field, which are alive today and burnt in the oven tomorrow, is he not much more likely to clothe you, you 'little-faiths'? . . . [Y]our Heavenly Father knows that you need them all. *Set your heart first on his kingdom and his goodness, and all these things will come to you as a matter of course* (Matt. 6:25–34, PHILLIPS, emphasis added).

THE QUALITIES OF A GOOD PROBLEM SOLVER

Good problem solvers are marked by certain qualities. The first quality may be *enthusiasm*. I have a friend, Peb Jackson, who is the most enthusiastic person I've ever known. Faced with a very complex schedule and sometimes overwhelming difficulties, he is often heard to say, "No problem" and "Not to worry." His enthusiasm is contagious, and his attitude toward problems is amazing and infectious. I have rarely, if ever, seen him worry. Someone once said, "Worry often gives a small thing a big shadow." Peb has the ability of making mountains into mole hills and getting problems down to fighting size. His faith serves him well, but his daily faith is a matter of choice. Don't assume that Peb is without problems. He isn't. No one is. Yet Peb chooses to approach problems aggressively, creatively, and enthusiastically.

A second vital quality is confidence. Rudy Markmiller, a profound Christian friend and founder-president of Network Courier, exudes a humble but indefatigable confidence. I've never seen him intimidated by a problem. He approaches each directly and objectively, but he is also creative and never accepts easy answers. At the same time, he doesn't unnecessarily complicate his situations. He is one of the finest problem solvers I've ever encountered.

So if enthusiasm and confidence are important qualities for good problem solving what are some of the others? Good problem solvers:

- *have confidence in their ability to learn and their ability to solve problems.*

- *tend to enjoy solving problems.*
- *rely on their own judgment.* Though they know there is wisdom in much counsel, they respect their own decision-making abilities.
- *are not fearful of being wrong or of making mistakes.*
- *are not fast answerers.* Although they don't procrastinate on decisions, they don't make hasty decisions either. Before making any decision, they gather as much data as they can.
- *are flexible and are often capable of seeing more than one answer to a question or a problem.*
- *know the difference between fact and opinion, and have a high degree of respect for fact.*
- *do not need to have an absolute, final, irrevocable solution to every problem.* They know that the only thing that is constant is change.

Julien Phillips works for McKensey and Co., the group that inspired the best-selling book *In Search of Excellence* by Tom Peters and Bob Waterman. He travels throughout the world consulting with companies on how they can improve their organizations. He works with incredible complexities, yet he has the ability to utilize all the above principles and more in making decisions and offering fresh insights to executives. One of his unique abilities is the art of designing and asking penetrating questions. Those questions enable companies throughout the world to grow, even beyond their hopes and expectations. He is an absolutely exquisite problem solver because he is always open to new possibilities.

YOU DON'T HAVE TO BE PERFECT

Edwin Bliss once said, "The pursuit of excellence is gratifying and healthy. The pursuit of perfection is frustrating, neurotic, and a terrible waste of time." While all of us would love to be potent problem solvers, like the three men mentioned above, we must realize it takes time, effort, discipline, practice, study, and prayer to accomplish our goals. I recently saw a tremendous formula for success. It consists of these ten points:

1. Pray
2. Work

3. Pray
4. Work
5. Pray
6. Work
7. Pray
8. Work
9. Pray
10. Work

All of us should remember that none of the techniques suggested in this book is intended to be a substitute for the incredible power of Christ in our lives. If you want to improve your problem-solving abilities, follow all ten suggestions. But in the process of developing our problem-solving skills, we've got to be careful of the trap of perfectionism. Somebody once said that "perfectionism leads to procrastination, and procrastination in turn leads to paralysis." One of the things that will paralyze us most in the process of becoming better problems solvers is striving for immediate perfection. Yes, pay attention to detail. Yes, pursue excellence. But avoid that nagging tendency to strive for perfection, especially on the first attempt.

Babe Ruth struck out 1,330 times, yet was considered one of the greatest baseball players of all time. Thomas Edison, one of this country's most famous inventors, discovered at least 1,800 ways *not* to make a light bulb. Columbus thought he was finding a shortcut to India. Johannes Kepler stumbled on to the idea of interplanetary gravity because of assumptions which were right for the wrong reasons.

Roger Von Oech tells of a conversation with the creative director of an advertising agency who said he wasn't happy unless he was failing at least half the time. As he put it, "If you're going to be original, you are going to be wrong a lot."[5]

---

[5] Roger Von Oech, *A Whack on the Side of the Head: How to Unlock Your Mind for Innovation* (New York: Warner Books, 1983).

I LOVE A CHALLENGE

Your attitude does not depend upon circumstances, personality, IQ, education, or genealogy. It does not depend upon how many degrees you have, or how many Bible verses you memorize. It depends solely upon the choices you make each day about each and every problem you face. It demands courage and practice.

When Sherry Leonard was young, she contracted muscular dystrophy. At one point in her life, she struggled so much with it and her despair was so deep that she contemplated suicide. After she encountered Jesus Christ, she realized she had a choice about what her outlook would be. I met Sherry a few years ago on a Summit Expedition *Go-For-It* program for the physically handicapped. One can't be around her for more than a few minutes without realizing that this young person is in love with life, in love with God and thinks that each day is a very special gift to be enjoyed and to be shared.

Sherry's joy is radiant. Her self-esteem is perhaps the soundest I have ever seen, not only in a handicapped person but in any young person I have ever met. She enjoys being Sherry Leonard, even though she will never be able to walk, even though she has to use one arm to lift the other. Life can be very difficult for her at times, but the most dominant characteristic about Sherry Leonard is her attitude.

She is beautiful not only on the outside but especially on the inside. When you see her smile, you know that smile comes from the very core of her being. She chooses each day to make it that way. As we returned from our challenging wilderness experience, she said, "Muscular dystrophy is my gift from God." She went on to explain how it gives her the opportunity to share her relationship with Jesus Christ. I was humbled to think of the many times I have complained about some of the puny problems and pains that I've had to endure. Her zest for life and God is contagious.

Last year, Sherry was one of the first *Go-For-It* participants ever to rappel off of the "Prow," one of the most dangerous and difficult cliffs in our wilderness program. A 150-foot rappel, it requires hanging free from the rock most of the way down, until you arrive at a 6- to 10-foot edge where you can walk off. When you rappel there, you can look down almost 1,000 feet. It's something very few people can handle. For Sherry, it was a challenge that she couldn't wait to take on.

In a recent letter, she wrote: "Dearest Timbo, How are you doing, big guy? I am doing *terrific* as usual . . ." She starts every letter that way. She went on to talk about how excited she was to be in *Go-For-It* again. She said she was thrilled to have the opportunity to work full time now and how anxious she was to be able to share her life with young people through the ministry of Young Life. She ended the letter by saying, "It can be a little inconvenient at times, but I always did *love* a challenge!!!"

Part 2

Principles: How to Keep the Elephants off Your Airhose

Introduction: The Ten Commendments of Problem Solving

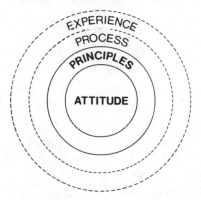

God made us, and God is able to empower us to do whatever he calls us to do. Denying that we can accomplish God's work is not humility; it is the worst kind of pride!

Warren Wiersbe

The message from the moon . . . is that no problem need any longer be considered unsolvable.

Norman Cousins

A principle is a short statement based on long experience.

The following chapters, which I have for fun gathered under the label "The Ten Commendments of Problem Solving," are designed to provide you with the necessary tools for unlocking your imagination and your problem-solving abilities. There is no special order or sequence to them. These "commendments" (that is, suggestions or recommendations) are fluid and should be used as needed. These are the principles of problem solving that I use at problem-solving seminars.

A principle provides you with "a place to begin." As condensed truth, principles provide concrete expressions of reality-based-on-experience. They are compressed ideas with the density of distillation and the gravity of experience. In essence they're a "weighted" axiom that can provide ballast for us when we approach a problem-solving situation.

Principles are not magic formulas or recipes. They are not shortcuts, not necessarily "rules," not laws you must obey, not restrictions, not "absolutes," or guarantees. Principles are tools, but tools are useless if they remain on the shelf. Thus principles may provide inspiration—but we must add to them our own perspiration. Their effectiveness depends on how you use them. The ten principles of problem solving are as follows:

1. Challenge assumptions.
2. Keep a broad perspective.
3. Don't get hooked.
4. Simple is better.
5. Look for a second right answer.
6. Ask dumb questions.
7. Unlock your creativity.
8. Scratch where it itches.
9. Make it fun!
10. Hang in there.

In the wilderness, we use a map and compass as navigational tools. Your skill in using these tools determines whether or not you get lost. In the same way, these principles are navigational tools . . . the more you use them, the better you'll get at solving problems.

The problem-solving journey is not a somber, joyless procession. Instead, it is a dance, a parade, something closer to a Mardi Gras than a forced march. Studies have shown that you and I tend to enjoy doing what we are good at. Likewise, we are good at doing what we enjoy. Therefore, problem solving like all other skills takes practice in order to become enjoyable. In order to maximize your understanding and use of these principles, try to solve some of the exercises included with each principle. I think you will find them both challenging and amusing. Enjoy the process and have fun.

4

Challenge Assumptions

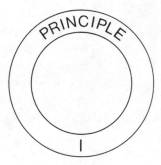

Gentlemen, we're surrounded by insurmountable opportunities.

Pogo

Our making assumptions creates perhaps the biggest obstacle to creative problem solving. On the one hand, assumptions are a great energy saving device. As we move through life we learn from past experiences and, hence, can anticipate what to expect in certain situations and respond accordingly.

If, for example, having a cup of coffee after dinner has kept you awake at bedtime for the last four nights, you can assume that if you have coffee with dinner tonight, you will probably have some difficulty sleeping. So, in certain situations our assumptions can be of help.

In problem solving, however, they can frequently pull our thinking in the wrong direction. In our Summit Expedition courses we use a variety of experiences and exercises to challenge participants to let go of their assumptions and to think more clearly about their lives and their beliefs.

• A famous surgeon was about to operate on a child who had been in an accident. The doctor, upon examining the child exclaimed, "I can't operate on this boy. He's my son!"

However, the surgeon was not the boy's father. How can you explain this?

• A man lives on the top floor of a twelve-story apartment building. Each morning on his way to work, he gets in the elevator and pushes the button for the first floor. When he gets to the bottom he gets off the elevator, takes a subway to the office, and returns home at 5:30 each evening. He then gets on the elevator, pushes the button for the third floor, and then gets off and walks up to the top floor. *Question:* Why does he do this?

• Here is another quite famous example, sometimes called a "minute mystery." You enter a room. There you find Fred and Martha lying dead on the floor amidst broken glass and water. A cat is running out of the room. How did they die? Remember: Challenge your assumptions.

• Finally, here is an exercise of a different variety. What you have is a Roman numeral 9:

IX

Can you add only one line to make it into a 6? (See if you can come up with a second and a third way to do it.)

How are you doing so far? If you are like most of us and these simple solutions elude you, you've probably made certain assumptions.

We all tend to make assumptions. They are not only the most common difficulty in problem solving, but also the easiest mistakes to make because we continually have to make assumptions in order to navigate our way through everyday life.

To assume is to think that you already know. What some people call "thinking" is simply a rearranging of their prejudices—but in problem solving making assumptions is like rearranging the deck chairs on the *Titanic*. Assumptions result from limited information or from looking at a problem from the wrong angle. Oftentimes, assumptions are faulty interpretations of the given facts, frequently occurring when we look only on the surface of things.

Moses *assumed* that God couldn't use someone who stuttered and almost detoured one of the greatest events of the Old Testament. Elijah *assumed* that "he was the only believer left." The people around David *assumed* that a young boy with no armor didn't stand a chance against a nine-foot giant. (Fortunately, David didn't make the same assumption!) Gideon *assumed* he wasn't a warrior and couldn't do what God called him to do. The list could go on and on.

In our everyday life, we, too, make constant assumptions. When we come to certain problems we say "it's not logical," "it's not practical," "that's not my area," "I'm not creative," or "we've never done it that way before." Often we assume that "speaking is more important than listening," that "being busy is more important than being still," that "big is better than small," that "new is better than old," that "some place far away is better than right here," or that "fast is better than slow." Likewise, I know many people who assume that everyday life is boring, not realizing that in reality that's all we have.

In my life, to assume means that I'm not thinking creatively and critically, that I'm not seeing the big picture or the whole perspective, that I'm not basing what I believe on facts but on opinions. Assumptions, let me remind you again, are so common because making them is so easy. They are a natural overflow of our experience. Christians, I think, can be sometimes very susceptible to a multitude of assumptions. Because we look to God for guidance, we sometimes assume that there is "one" way to do things, that for certain situations there is one "right" answer.

When I was working with inner-city kids in New York, I was invited to a conference where a woman was speaking on the subject of missionaries. She asked a simple question, "What is a missionary?"

The kids' hands went up immediately, "Someone who has a mission."

The woman said, "No."

The next young person suggested, "Someone who goes overseas to share the gospel," to which the woman again replied no.

Someone else said, "A missionary is a person who helps translate the Bible into other languages." Her answer was still no. There must have been at least a dozen other answers that I thought were appropriate and good answers. Each time she answered them with a no, until she had completely squelched their curiosity and eagerness. Then in a very prim and proper way, she read her rather stale definition of what a missionary was. It was so boring that I can't even recall her words.

This was a tragedy. These kids had been so eager and enthusiastic, wanting to participate, and yet eventually so discouraged by this woman's preconceived assumption. I heard someone say recently what I thought was a rather profound insight: that a missionary is simply "someone who gets outside of himself."

What assumptions are you making that hamper your ability to solve problems creatively? Let's go back to the problems I gave you earlier. In the first exercise you were asked to explain how the surgeon would say "I can't operate, he's my son," and yet not be the boy's father. It is amazing how many people have difficulty with this exercise because of our stereotypes of doctors. We assume all doctors to be male, perhaps because we see so many male images in our media. The doctor, in fact, is the boy's mother. This is a good example of how our culture influences the assumptions we make. See how important it is for us to challenge our assumptions.

The second exercise had to do with the man who came home and pushed the button to the third floor and then walked up nine flights of stairs to get to his apartment. I remember when someone first challenged me with this riddle. I confess I didn't do too well, and in fact I had to laugh at myself when I discovered that he was a midget and, therefore, he couldn't reach beyond the third button.

The third exercise stands out quite vividly in my memory because I got locked onto some assumptions that literally made a fool out of me. Confident of my ability to ask good questions, when I was approached with the Fred-and-Martha-lying-dead-on-the-floor problem, I began to ask all sorts of questions. In fact, my questions went on for over an hour. The friend who had shared the riddle with me was by then laughing uproariously as my questions—and the answers—got more and more ludicrous. I remember toward the end asking questions like "Were Fred and Martha dressed normally?"

He said, "No."

I finally took a chance and said, "Did they have any clothes on at all?"

He said with a big smile, "No."

Then I began to explore what they must have looked like. I said, "Were they normal looking people?"

Laughing still harder, he said, "No."

I said, "Well, do they have arms and legs?"

By this time my friend had tears in his eyes from laughing so hard. He said, "No."

I was getting these terribly embarrassing images that I didn't know what to do with. I finally said, "Well, were they fairly old?"

He said, "Yes."

This created purely ridiculous mental images of two elderly people with no arms or legs, no clothes, lying on the floor in a puddle of water. Finally the absurdity of it all led me to ask my friend if Fred and Martha were people. Laughing, with tears running down his cheeks he managed to get out a "No."

If you struggled with this one, I just want you to know, that I did too. I also want to remind you to keep having fun and to keep your sense of humor alive. Fred and Martha were fish! The cat had knocked over the fishbowl so that Fred and Martha were lying on the floor amidst broken glass and water, and the cat was running out the door.

How did you do with the Roman numeral nine? Were you able to transform it into a six with only one line? Most people assume two things in this exercise. One, that the line is straight, and two, that the new number must still be a Roman numeral. Both of those are unnecessary assumptions. One of the ways, for example, to solve this problem is simply putting a wavy line in front of the IX—that is, spell out "SIX."

If you did get that, were you able to come up with a second or third possible answer? One of our students very cleverly did the following:

IX6

In this solution, the "X" becomes a multiplication symbol (x) and the "6" is a single line. It still uses only one line. Clever thinking. There may be other answers, too. The purpose of this book is to get you to stretch your thinking; the purpose of this section in particular is to encourage you to challenge some of your assumptions.

Here is a final illustration of what can happen when people allow themselves to break their assumptions. What do sandbags hold? Well, the answer is obviously sand. That's the reason they are called sandbags. In many areas of the United States, people line rivers with sandbags when they are in danger of a flood. The sandbags work to control the banks and hold the flooding river in its natural channel. However, sandbags are costly and cumbersome. Getting enough sand to a particular flood site can be a difficult problem.

Some years ago the Japanese developed a different solution to the problem. They were having trouble locating enough sand to fill the sandbags. Letting go of their preconceived assumptions that only sand can fill a sandbag, they devised bags which they fill with water. These "waterbags" were then stacked along the banks of the flooding river the same as sandbags are. They are just as effective at stopping flooding rivers, but they are much easier to use, they cost less, and they store more easily (when the water is emptied out).[1]

Challenging assumptions is perhaps one of the best ways to find a better solution to your problem.

------

[1] Kurt Hanks et al., *Design Yourself!* (Los Altos, Calif.: William Kauffman, 1977), 95.

5

Keep a Broad
Perspective

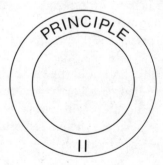

There is a great deal of unmapped country within us.

George Eliot

If the only tool you have is a hammer, you tend to see every
problem as a nail.

Abraham Maslow

Someone once said that the mind is like a parachute; it works best
when it's open. An American theologian doing research on Orien-
tal religions sought a certain brilliant Zen master for instruction.

The Zen master invited him one afternoon to tea. After the initial conversation, the Zen master asked the theologian if he would like some tea. When the theologian said yes, the Zen master began to pour the tea into his cup. The cup filled, but the Zen master continued to pour until the cup overflowed and spilled out onto the table. The theologian said, "Sir, you must stop pouring. I have more than enough. It's no longer going into the cup." The Zen master replied, "True indeed. You are very observant; however, the same is true with you. If you are to learn any of my teachings, you must first empty what you have in your mental cup."

Opening windows within yourself in turn opens countless possibilities in your situation. Many people suffer from what could rightly be called "a hardening of the categories." They aren't capable of seeing—or they refuse to see—the whole picture. Little do they realize that these self-imposed limitations greatly restrict their problem-solving abilities.

Keeping a broad perspective will definitely influence how you will approach a problem—and indeed, its final outcome. For example, consider the following drawing:

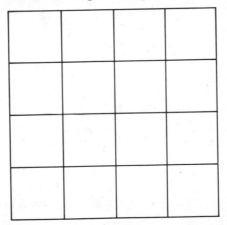

How many squares are there? Look carefully; don't limit your perspective.

If you said sixteen, you're right. However, if you said seventeen, you're also right. Perhaps you saw twenty, that's correct too. Maybe you even saw twenty-four. Outstanding. However, did you see all thirty? Many people give this problem a superficial look and see only sixteen squares. In fact, there are thirty. Note that sixteen is a little more than half of thirty. I am convinced that in nearly every problem situation we encounter, there is at least *twice* as much information—if not more—available to us than we normally perceive.

Learn how to look at problems from different angles. Ask tough questions. Flex and stretch your perspective. See all that is there—see the problem as it *really* is in all its fullness.

When I taught high school, I used to do an exercise where I would put a dot on a blank sheet of paper. Then I would walk down each aisle, showing the paper to each student. I would ask them all the same question, "What do you see?" I remember in one class, thirty-two consecutive students saying simply "a dot." None noticed the paper which it was on, or the person who was holding it, or, if you want your perspective to get even larger, the room in which the person was standing. Obviously you can extend this perspective even further.

When an exercise like this is shown to preschool children, they see all kinds of possibilities. You'll hear answers like, "a squashed mosquito," "a ladybug," "a period," or "a man's hat from the top." Young children, whose perspective has not yet been limited, tend to see all sorts of creative forms in a dot.

Is there perhaps a problem you're wrestling with now in which your perspective is limited? Are you using all the creative gifts that God has given you? Is there another way to look at the problem? Can you reframe it? Can you look at it from a larger perspective? In fact, can you see that problem from God's perspective? Many times being able to see our problems from God's perspective changes the situation entirely.

I'm always amazed at Paul's perspective on life. The Book of Philippians was written after Paul had been shipwrecked, stoned, and beaten. It was written from a prison, where Paul was chained to a Roman guard, and yet, in Philippians, he uses the words "joy" and "rejoice" more than nineteen times. The only way he could possibly do something like this was to view his problems from God's perspective. When he did that, he could say in effect, that his problems were an "advantage" to the gospel: "Now I want you to know, my brothers, that what has happened to me has, in effect, turned out to the advantage of the gospel" (Phil. 1:12, PHILLIPS).

Then two chapters later Paul makes a radical statement implying that our suffering is actually a privilege because it brings us into a deeper relationship with Jesus Christ. "Now I long to know Christ and the power shown by his resurrection; now I long to share his sufferings. . . . Not that I claim to have achieved this, nor to have reached perfection already. But I keep going on, trying to grasp that purpose for which Christ Jesus grasped me. My brothers, I do not consider myself to have grasped it fully even now. But I do concentrate on this: I forget all that lies behind me and with hands outstretched to whatever lies ahead I go straight for the goal—my reward, the honour of my high calling by God and Christ Jesus" (Phil. 3:13–14, PHILLIPS).

That is perspective! Paul considered his problems an advantage, and he realized that whatever happened had to be left behind. He reached forward eagerly to whatever the future held so that he could maintain his focus, that of deepening his relationship with Christ.

Many places in this letter to the Philippians remind us of what the possibilities of our perspective could be. Here's a man who had been absolutely overwhelmed with problems, yet he closes his letter by saying, "Now I have everything I want—in fact I am rich. Yes, I am quite content. . . . My God will supply all that you need from his glorious resources in Christ Jesus" (Phil. 4:18–19, PHILLIPS).

Paul continually reminds us to look at our lives and our problems from God's point of view. In the next book (his letter to the Christians at Colossae) he says, "We are asking God that you may see things, as it were, from his point of view by being given spiritual insight and understanding" (Col. 1:9, PHILLIPS*).

As I am working on this chapter, I received a letter from Alexa Knight, a relatively new friend. What amazing timing in that I was thinking about how we need to view our problems differently. In the middle of her letter she says, "No, unfortunately my problems didn't all disappear but some changes *have* happened. As a successful professional woman who has been single for twelve years, I was reminded (as I have been for years) that I try too hard to control and make things happen my way. I've again turned it all over to the Lord, but this time with perhaps a little more trust—*and some incredible things began to happen.*"

Like Alexa, I constantly need to be reminded to let go, to turn things over to Him, and to see my problems from His perspective.

Perspective has the potential to convert a problem into a hope. Our problems don't have to be just present problems either. Some of us still continue to carry guilt and heaviness over some problem in the past, and it weighs down our present. Seeing things from our limited perspective, we are sometimes unable to forgive ourselves and, hence, continue to block the beauty of what Thomas Merton called the "ever-occurring festival of present-ness."

I heard a story of a priest, who lived in the Philippines, who had a woman in his parish who deeply loved God. In fact, this woman claimed that at night she often had visions in which she talked with Christ and he talked with her. The priest, however, was skeptical of her claims, so to test her visions he said to her, "You say that you actually speak directly with Christ in your visions? Then let me ask you a favor. The next time you have one of these visions, I want you to ask Him what terrible sin your priest committed when he was in seminary."

The sin the priest spoke of was something he had done in secret, and no one knew except him and Christ. This sin, this years-old sin, however, was such a great burden of guilt to him that he was unable to freely experience joy or peace and was unable to free himself to live in the present. He wanted forgiveness, but felt he never could be forgiven.

The woman agreed to ask the priest's question in her next time of prayer and went home. When she returned to the church a few days later, the priest said, "Well, did Christ visit you in your dreams?"

"Yes, He did," replied the woman.

"And did you ask Him what sin I committed in seminary," he asked rather cynically.

"Yes, I asked Him."

"Well, what did He say?"

Then she quietly responded, "He said, 'I don't remember.'"[1]

As followers of Jesus Christ we need to realize that if we have confessed our sins to Him and have turned from them, they are past tense. They are over. The sins have not only been forgiven, but forgotten. "I am He who blots out your transgressions for my own sake, and I will not remember your sins" (Isa. 43:25, RSV; but look also at Jer. 31:34; Heb. 8:12; 10:17).

WHY ME? OR WHY ME?

It all depends on your perspective.

Myopia is a disease of the eyes which makes one near-sighted. Myopia can also be a disease of the spirit which sometimes afflicts us all. In the midst of a problem we become so preoccupied with ourselves that we cannot fully comprehend the situation. I read a story recently in the paper of a man who, while intoxicated, drove his car into a group of students, killing two and injuring several more. When he got out of the car and surveyed the situation, the first thing he said was, "Why *me*? Why *me*?" He was so preoccupied with himself that he couldn't see the real catastrophe around him.

---

[1] Ron Lee Davis, *Gold in the Making* (Nashville: Thomas Nelson, 1984), 86.

All of us are in danger of this at one time or another. In fact the "why me" syndrome seems to be something of a contagious disease. Yet gaining the proper perspective on a situation is the quickest remedy for the "why me" syndrome. Consider the following two examples.

On one of our recent *Go-For-It* programs (Summit Expedition's wilderness program for the physically handicapped) I was having a bad day. I live with chronic pain as a result of a climbing accident in 1974, and I felt as if I had a migraine all over my body. My mind was drifting off into the "why me" mentality when I looked over and saw Pam Dahl, one of our students.

Because she was deprived of two minutes of oxygen at birth, Pam Dahl lives with severe cerebral palsy. She has never walked; she has never been able to lift her hands from her lap, so she has never known what it means to brush her hair or to eat a meal by herself. The cerebral palsy has also somewhat impaired her speech. Yet as I watched her, I saw a most radiant kind of joy. Her smile was one of the most beautiful I'd ever seen. She was getting ready to take on her first rock-climbing challenge.

Although she has never been able to stand, with the help of some of our instructors, she tied onto the rope at the bottom of the cliff. For the next hour and a half she inched her way up the rock to the marvel of us all.

I've seen some of the greatest rock climbers in the world take on difficult, almost impossible climbs, but I have to confess that Pam Dahl's climb was the greatest climb I'd ever seen in my life. She displayed a quality of courage that most of us never even dream of. Her excitement overwhelmed the pain and the difficulty. When she got to the top, some instructors helped her over to a nearby rock where she curled up her bent legs underneath her and with her hands still pinned to her lap, she looked at us and said, "That was fun. Let's do it again."

Needless to say, I became rather embarrassed about my recent "pity party."

Changing our perspective sets us free to see problems as they really are.

One day, the parents of a college student received a letter from their daughter which went something like this:

Dear Mom and Dad,

Just thought I'd drop you a note to clue you in on my plans. I've fallen in love with a guy named Jim. He quit high school after the eleventh grade to get married. It didn't work out and he's been divorced now about a year. Jim and I have been going together for two months and we plan to get married in the fall. Until then I've decided to move into his apartment.

I hate to say it, but I'm also having a problem with drugs. (By the way, I think that I might be pregnant.) At any rate, I dropped out of school last week, although I'd really like to finish college sometime in the future.

The young woman's parents anxiously turned to page two of their daughter's letter:

Mom and Dad, I just want you to know that everything I've written so far is *false*. Not a word of it is true. But it is true that I got a C– in French and that I flunked a math test. I just wanted to put things in perspective.

THE CATASTROPHE PRINCIPLE

One of the most useful techniques I've learned in helping to put things in their proper perspective is what I call the "catastrophe principle." What you do is stretch out the long-term consequences of the problem you're dealing with to its most distant conclusion. In other words, say to yourself, "What is the worst possible thing that could happen in this situation?" For example: if I didn't complete this book, the worst thing that could happen would be that my publisher would drop me as an author. I wouldn't like for that to happen, but let's suppose it did. After imagining the worst possible situation I ask myself, "Could I live with this consequence?" Yes, I could. By imagining things in this way I realize that life is more than a publishing contract. God would open up other opportunities. I would survive the situation.

Once we have faced the full impact of our worst catastrophe and decided that we can live through it, we are free to face anything along the way. The catastrophe principle is a good way of putting our problems into proper perspective.

MASTER THINKING

Jesus speaks to us in Matt. 6:22–23 about perspective: "The eye is the lamp of the body. If your eyes are good, your whole body will be full of light. But if your eyes are bad, your whole body will be full of darkness. If then the light within you is darkness, how great is that darkness!" (NIV).

Are you filling your life "full of darkness" because your vision is too short-sighted? Are you only allowing yourself a limited view of your present circumstances and of yourself? Perhaps you are in danger of becoming the powerless victim of your problems. There is a life-changing solution. It's not an easy solution, but it promises unimaginable power and freedom. Jesus says in Matt. 6:31–32, "So do not worry, saying, 'What shall we eat?' or 'What shall we drink?' or 'What shall we wear?' For the pagans run after these things, and your heavenly Father knows that you need them. *But seek first his kingdom and his righteousness, and all these things will be given to you as well*" (NIV, emphasis added).

We are asked to see beyond our own limited resources and opinions and to see our circumstances with the eyes of God. You may not find this difficult, but I certainly do. This means I must trust God's judgment about what my family needs to flourish and grow. It means I must trust God with a great deal more than I can afford to lose. It means I must realize that my abilities to provide for those I care for are fragile unless secured by the Father's love. Yet once I recognize God's providence, He transfigures all my impossibilities into attainable goals. Whole new vistas open up, we see from a whole new vantage point, and we are never the same because of what we have seen.

6

Don't Get "Hooked"

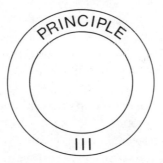

A hysteric is a person who has discovered the secret of perpetual emotion.

Emotions should be servants, not masters—or at least not tyrants.

Rodger H. Benson

All emotions are pure which gather you and lift you up. That emotion is impure which seizes only one side of your being—and so distorts you.

Ranier Maria Rilke

Consider the following letters:

O T T F F S S

What are the next three letters?

E N T

That's right! It's as simple as counting, isn't it? What are the next five letters?

E T T F F

Have you got it? It's as simple as 1-2-3, isn't it?

Can you tell by now what the next letters are going to be? I'm sure you've got it by now. It's one of the first patterns you ever learned, wasn't it?

Okay. What letters come next? If you said S S E N T T T T T T T T T T T T T, you're absolutely right!

In my problem-solving seminars, at least a few people have recognized the pattern by this point. When I say, "It's very simple, isn't it?" they laughingly affirm a big yes—which absolutely *exasperates* the rest of the group. "How old were you when you first learned this pattern?" I ask someone who understands the pattern.

He or she usually responds, "Oh, about three or four years old."

Then those who know it chat and laugh. At this point I usually ask the rest of them, "How many of you would like to punch my lights out about now?" Scores of hands raise furiously. For some, frustration has turned into anger. Then I ask, "How many of you 'don't give a rip' what the next letter is?" This also usually gets more than a few hands (remember, frustration begets anger, which begets apathy).

You've got it by now, right? The next letters could only be T T T T T T F F F F. It should be obvious by now.

By the way, how are your emotions at this point? How are you doing? More precisely, how are you *feeling*? Have you gotten emotionally hooked by all of this—like so many of the seminar participants did? If you have, what effect do you think your feelings have had on your problem-solving capabilities? When I ask in the seminars, the answers are usually something like this:

- My abilities are reduced to zero.
- I'm so mad I can't even think straight.
- I'm so frustrated that I don't care anymore.
- I've reduced my problem-solving abilities to a pinpoint.
- I'm paralyzed.
- I'm simply not effective anymore.

It really is a simple pattern. But in another sense it could look very complex. In case you still haven't got it, the next letters are as follows:

F F F F F F F F F F F F F F F
S S S S S

If you think you're about to go crazy at this point, check the answers at the end of this chapter. You'll find it simpler than you thought it was. (This is, by the way, a great one to try on your friends.)

Getting emotionally hooked is one of the easiest, most common, and most dangerous facets of problem solving. None of us is immune to it. We've all succumbed to our emotions at one point or another, and we will again—probably soon.

Emotions are good. They're wonderful. Life would hardly be worth living without them. Living in an emotional vacuum would be dull, boring, and bland. But emotions also have the power to disrupt our lives seriously when we allow them to control us.

What do I mean by getting emotionally hooked? You're probably emotionally hooked when your emotions are in control, when you can no longer think logically. You're probably emotionally hooked when you try to make the other person "wrong" or you give "you" messages rather than "I" messages:

"You never liked my mother."

"The Boss is always picking on me."

"He's so stupid that . . ."

"That's my _____ you're talking about" (could be mother, child, job, achievement or anything else).

You are "hooked" when your emotions dominate and flood your thinking or when you're more concerned about your feelings than you are about the problem. In fact, when we're emotionally hooked, we often don't care any more about the problem. We simply want to satisfy our feelings.

For example, you are probably emotionally hooked if you could have no greater pleasure than seeing your boss's picture on the back of a milk carton. Another good sign that you're hooked is when you use words like "always" and "never"; you state your point in exaggerations and generalizations; you magnify the problem way out of proportion; you want emotional satisfaction more than a solution to the problem.

One night a friend of mine came home so mad he "could hardly see straight." When his wife asked him what was wrong, he testified, "Everything went wrong today! It took six years to get to work this morning because of some guy who decided to change his tire in the middle of the freeway. When I finally got to work, who is standing in my office, but Gerald, the sales manager? The man is brain dead. He spends every waking moment standing in my office asking me questions about things that have been in my memos for years. On top of that, the whole, entire production line blew up today, and it took me three hours to get them back on-line. I've never had a day like this. This has been the absolute worst day of my life!"

His wife exclaimed, "What are you so upset for? This is great!"

"What are you talking about?" was my friend's irritated response.

"With what you have discovered today, we'll be set for life!" his wife rejoined.

"I don't think I know what your talking about," said her puzzled husband.

"You're so modest. Do you realize that in one day you've managed to discover time travel, to get complex cognitive responses from a man with no brainwaves—though you really should get someone to take him home nights so he doesn't scare the cleaning ladies—and to repair an entire factory in three hours. You're absolutely brilliant!"

My friend laughed at the mental picture of Gerald standing in a dark, deserted office perpetually asking questions to a terrified cleaning crew. Perspective has more than a little to do with how emotionally hooked we get.

Unfortunately, there is a much darker side to being emotionally hooked. I have seen people who are so hooked that they refuse to speak to each other. Such actions are indicators of deep-seated anger and frustration. It doesn't take an Einstein to realize that the problem can't be solved—or even identified—if you are so emotionally paralyzed that you abandon both the problem and the people involved.

When you are emotionally hooked, you imprison yourself within a very narrow view of the problem. This takes on tragic consequences when the problem is perceived as a person. You can too easily forget all the good things about that person. Instead of being an opportunity for growth, the problem becomes a magnet pulling all your energy into a vacuum. You are unable to perceive or understand the other person's position, emotions, or pain.

Sometimes we lash out at the other person. Nathaniel Brandon once said, "No one has ever talked himself (or anyone else) out of an undesired emotion by hurling insults or by delivering a moral lecture." When you become emotionally hooked, you become the victim of your emotions and of your problems. You drain so much energy from the real problem, you distract your focus so much, you become so concerned about what's happening to you that you no longer care what the problem really is.

Let me hasten to add that I have never met anybody who hasn't had the repeated experience of getting emotionally hooked. That's one of the reasons for including this principle. The apostle Peter got emotionally hooked on many occasions; for example, slashing the guard's ear at Jesus' arrest certainly didn't solve the problem.

Carl Rogers, the famous psychologist, once said something that we all need to remember, "The *only* person who cannot be helped is that person who blames others." Once you blame others, you have given up the power to change. A problem cannot and will not be solved until the person involved accepts full responsibility for it and stops blaming others.

So what are some of the things we can do to avoid getting emotionally hooked? First, distance yourself from the problem. Go for a walk, get some exercise, back away from the problem until you can see it from a more detached point of view. Talk to a friend who is not in any way involved in the problem and have him or her help you find a proper perspective for the problem.

The Bible is an excellent place to turn to while trying to distance yourself emotionally from a problem. Excellent passages for this are found in Psalms and Ephesians. In my own times of trouble, I turn to Isa. 26:3, where the prophet says, "Thou wilt keep *him* in perfect peace, *whose* mind *is* stayed *on Thee.*"

When we are emotionally hooked, we need to focus (1) on God and His perspective on the problem and (2) on trying to find out what the problem really is. Try also to think about the problem as if it weren't your problem. That tends to lower your worry quotient. There's truth in the old saying, "give only a quarter's worth of worry to a quarter's worth of problem." One of the worst tragedies about worry is that it's so contagious and affects others so easily.

One of the best things you can do when you're emotionally hooked is to begin to focus on the components of the problem-solving process and ask yourself, "What is my attitude toward this problem . . . What are some of the major principles I can apply to this problem . . . How do I apply a logical, seven-step problem-solving process to this situation?

It is a good rule never to make an important decision when your emotions are in control. Postpone that decision until you are more relaxed and can think more clearly. I have some friends who have made a rule for their marriage that they never argue sex, religion, or politics after 9:00 P.M. They do that because they know that when they're fatigued, they're far more susceptible to getting emotionally hooked on volatile issues.

Mark's gospel says that "He arose and rebuked the wind, and said to the sea, 'Peace, be still!' And the wind ceased and there was a great calm" (Mark 4:39, NKJV). The Bible also reminds us that God is the same yesterday, today, and tomorrow. I am quite convinced that if He could calm the raging sea, He also has the ability to calm the tumult within us.

> A great many people are trying to 'make' peace, but that has already been done. God has not left it for us to do; all we have to do is enter into it.
>
> *Dwight L. Moody*

Relax. Trust. Let go. Look at your problem from another angle. Talk it over with a friend. Talk it over with The Friend. If you really want to get radical—thank Him for your problem. "Don't worry over anything whatever; whenever you pray tell God every *detail* of your needs in *thankful* prayer, and the peace of God, which surpasses human understanding, will keep constant guard over your hearts and minds as they *rest* in Christ Jesus" (Phil. 4:6–7, PHILLIPS).

Answer to O-T-T-F-F-S-S pattern: Each letter represents the first letter of the numbers as they're spelled out in the sequence: One, Two, Three, Four, Five, Six, and so on. When you get into the twenties and thirties, you get a string of T's followed by one of F's and S's. It *is* as simple as counting, isn't it?

7

Simple Is Better

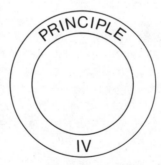

The greatest truths are the simplest—and so are the greatest men.

Augustus Hare

The ability to simplify means to eliminate the unnecessary so that the necessary may speak.

Hans Hoffman

At the beginning of most of our Summit Expedition courses, students participate in a series of warm-up problem-solving exercises which we call "initiative exercises." I remember in one situation giving a group of very bright students a problem called "The Electric Fence."

The "fence" is a piece of rope strung between two trees, approximately six feet high. The students are given a number of items, including a long pole, some carabiners,[1] some rope, some webbing, and a piece of cloth.

The group has to figure out a way to get everyone over the "electric fence." If they touch the rope, they will be "electrocuted."

It's a tremendous exercise that demonstrates a lot about creativity, problem solving, and leadership styles. Often participants make immediate assumptions about whom the leaders are supposed to be. I watched a group one time where a young girl immediately came up with a workable solution, but she was ignored. About fifteen minutes later a big, charismatic kid made the same proposal, and the group "discovered" the solution.

What was particularly humorous about this situation was that after they had correctly used the pole as a bridge over the fence, the self-imposed leader kept insisting that they hadn't solved the problem yet (even though they were all safely on the other side) because they hadn't used all the equipment.

Ironically, part of this problem-solving exercise was to teach them to eliminate unnecessary items in solving the problem. We had a tremendous discussion afterward.

Keep this exercise in mind when you face problems. There is equal danger in underdefining a problem as there is in overdefining it.

Simple answers are not necessarily simplistic answers. Band-aids are a simple, effective solution for cuts and scrapes, but they don't do a thing for cancer. Likewise simplistic answers don't address the real issues of a problem. If you use them, you will probably cover up what you don't understand rather than take the time to see the problem clearly. Therefore, you won't know enough about the problem to be able to sort the necessary from the unnecessary.

To simplify a problem means simply to remove that which clutters up your thinking.

- Here's another problem. Standing on a hard floor, figure out a way to drop an egg three feet without breaking it. This problem

---

[1] D-shaped rings used for fastening ropes in mountain climbing.

has stumped many individuals until they realized that the simplest answer is the best.

Robert Browning believed that less is more. Rudyard Kipling said, "Teach us to delight in simple things." When we reduce the complexity of problems by eliminating the extraneous, then the length of our problem-solving process is also reduced. In an article in *Design* magazine, Colin Carmichael tells the story of a class of engineering students who were given the following problem:

How long should a three-pound beef roast stay in a 325-degree oven for the center to reach a temperature of 150 degrees?

One student, described as a "big project man" didn't come up with an answer but did outline a series of experiments that would yield an accurate answer in six to nine months. A second student, more interested in practice than theory, went out and bought a roast, an oven thermometer, a meat thermometer, and a watch. He wrote up his report while snacking on medium-rare roast beef sandwiches. A third student reasoned that the specific heat conductivity of the roast should be similar to that of water, since water is the major element in animal tissue. He proved his hypothesis by applying heat transfer theory, and his results agreed closely with those of the second student. However, the quickest and most accurate answer came from the fourth student who simply called his mother and asked, "Hey Mom, how long do you cook a roast?"

Simple is better. The more complicated a problem, the greater the possibility of errors. Impressive answers that often dazzle the listener, sometimes do not solve the real problem. Take, for example, the classic drawing on the facing page that has been circulated in educational institutions for some time.

Today's business climate is complex, yet some of the best business solutions are the simplest. Tom Peters—one of the authors of *In Search of Excellence* and a popular business consultant—is often accused of discovering the obvious. He may offer deceptively simple answers, but his book has sold more than 5 million copies.

Likewise Buck Rogers, the thirty-four-year veteran executive of IBM who led that company's growth from $250 million to

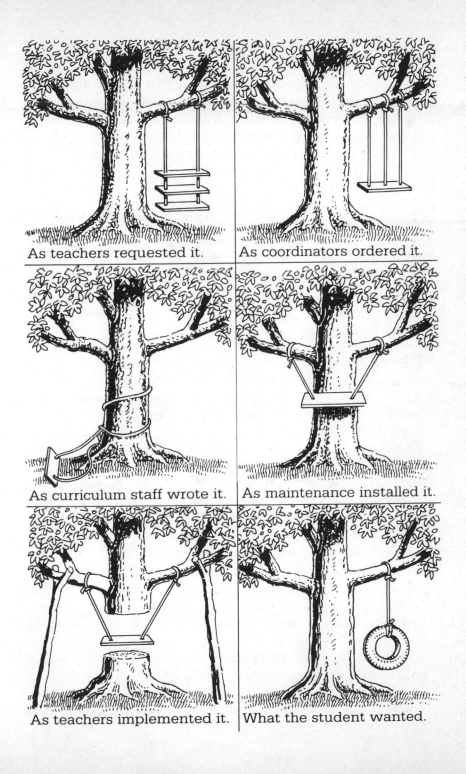

As teachers requested it.

As coordinators ordered it.

As curriculum staff wrote it.

As maintenance installed it.

As teachers implemented it.

What the student wanted.

$50 billion, recently wrote a book called *The IBM Way*. When it was reviewed, the critics said, "We should have known that Rogers would not really let us in on the real secrets of IBM." Rogers laughed at the criticism, saying, "I did tell what was at the heart of IBM. It's just so simple that a lot of people have a hard time believing it." He said, "There are no special secrets. We've just learned how to do the simple things well."

There is no good reason for making life more difficult than it needs to be. By complicating an issue, we often perceive that the amount of time, energy, and expertise required to solve a problem is greater than we can muster. But if we seek simpler, better-refined definitions of the problem first, we can often make unsolvable problems solvable. This is not only true for difficult situations, but also for difficult people.

KNOW THE COMPONENTS OF YOUR PROBLEM

What are the necessary components of the problems you're facing? Do you know your problem well enough to simplify it without succumbing to simplistic thinking? One of the benefits of living in a realistic community with mature people who know you well is that help is available to reduce problems to their simplest form. Other viewpoints help you to avoid personal prejudices and help unlock your thinking. Even when no ready answers are available, simply having someone's support makes a world of difference.

Pam and I went out to dinner at a time in my life when I seemed to have one crisis on top of another. I was feeling overwhelmed by the number and complexity of problems I had to face. My problems had problems. As we were having our salad I began to vent some of my frustrations. My wife took the simplest and most profound approach: she listened. For ten to fifteen minutes she simply listened intently to my struggles. Then at the end she said, "Babe, I don't blame you for being frustrated. If I had to deal with all those things I'd be frustrated too."

Her listening combined with that simple encouragement seemed to erase 80 percent of my problems. I left dinner that evening feeling rejuvenated and able to take on all that I had to face. She has taught me over the years that when someone has a problem they don't necessarily want you to fix it for them. They simply want someone to listen.

Simplicity is often the mark of wisdom. Many of our problems would disappear if we had a single standard by which we made our decisions. Charles Sheldon wrote *In His Steps* in 1897, and tells the story of a group of townspeople who had such a standard. At each intersection of life, these people would simply ask, "What would Jesus do?" This was a serious question to them, and they vowed not to make any decisions without first asking it. The results were— and are—nothing short of revolutionary.

When Calvin Bruce, a minister from Chicago, came to study the situation, his conscience led him to make radical changes in both his personal life and in his ministry. He feared, however, the reactions of his affluent congregation.

The Reverend Calvin Bruce writes in a report to a fellow minister in New York: "My church is wealthy, full of well-to-do, satisfied people. The standard of their discipleship is, I am aware, not of a nature to respond to the call of suffering or personal loss. . . . Shall I go back to my people next Sunday and stand up before them in my large city church and say: 'Let us follow Jesus closer; let us walk in His steps where it will cost us something more than it is costing us now; let us pledge not to do anything without first asking: What would Jesus do?'"

Charles Sheldon writes that "Calvin Bruce, D.D., went back to Chicago, and the great crisis in his Christian life in the ministry suddenly broke irresistibly upon him."

It is one of the signs of the kingdom of Heaven among us that the simple can result in profound change.

I can vividly remember a Bible study with a group of high-school students from Sequoia High School in the San Francisco area. We had been examining the basic theology and doctrine of the church. We'd been exploring the philosophical and theological positions of the church through history, debating the relevance of each to today's immense problems of hunger, nuclear weapons, and other ultra-complex situations. We had been exploring how their subjects at school wove together with all the subtleties of Scripture.

We talked some about the Greek and Hebrew roots of some of our words, a little about hermeneutics, and a little about ontology. Finally one morning a student raised her hand and said, "I'm really getting confused. Is it okay when I get lost in all of this stuff—*if I just look at Jesus?*"

The older I get the more dignity, elegance, and power I see in simplicity. I am discovering that the truly deep people have at the core of their being the genius of being simple. Their inner and outer lives seem to match. They are available, uncluttered, and open. They have a oneness with life.

Albert Einstein was famous for his admiration of childlike simplicity. Through his immense powers of wonder and concentration, he changed the world with a simple formula: $E = mc^2$. This formula reminds me of Richard Foster's statement, "Simplicity is not really simple."

To look at Jesus, to understand from the gospels how He lived, and live by the commands He gave us is not very complicated. "Love your neighbor as yourself," "love God with all your heart, soul, and mind," "as I have loved you, so you must love one another"—it's really pretty straight-forward. In fact, it's simple! But it isn't easy.

If we are wise, our journey through life will be toward that profound simplicity that triumphs over confusion. "To be simple" Dietrich Bonhoeffer said, "is to fix one's eyes solely on the simple truth of God at a time when all concepts are being confused, distorted, and turned up-side down. It means to be single-hearted."

Chris Slagle told me an anecdote that illustrates the importance of this singularity of purpose. Like all college students, when he was in college, Chris had numerous problems. One evening he phoned Dave, a friend of his who was older and wiser, and asked if he could visit to discuss some of his problems. Dave said yes. Chris got in his old, beat-up car and, with a lot of coaxing, made it to Dave's house.

Chris was eager to share some of his problems with Dave, knowing that Dave with all of his experience and wisdom would have much to offer. Chris was wrestling with four major problems. One, a girlfriend problem. Two, whether he should stay in school or go to work. Three, whether he should sell his car. Four, whether he should move back to Chicago where his family lived. Chris laid out these problems with a great deal of intricacy and emotion. He stressed again and again how important each of these problems was and, thus, how significant his decisions would be. He emphasized how much it would mean to him if Dave could help him move toward some resolution.

Dave walked over to a nearby table, picked up a Bible, brought it back and read Matt. 6:33 to Chris: "But seek first his kingdom and his righteousness, and all these things shall be yours as well" (RSV).

Chris thanked him for reading that verse and then began elaborating again on each of his problems, carefully explaining the ramifications of his different options. Again he asked Dave for his insight into these difficulties. Once more Dave picked up the Scripture and read Matt. 6:33. Chris became impatient and said something like, "Yeah, yeah, yeah, okay, that's great. Now, regarding the college situation. . . ." Again Dave read Matt. 6:33. Chris finally realized that no other answer was forthcoming, so he got in his car and left. He smoldered for the next three days. Finally, however, it dawned on him that what Dave had read was really true. He began understanding how this "simple" verse could place his problems in a whole new light.

Life is bewildering for many of us. Our problems can become so perplexing that they often mystify us. Even everyday living in our modern time can be puzzling. Perhaps simplicity has to do with adherence to truth. Perhaps it will always be a constant search, a direction in which we are hopefully moving.

Simplicity does not necessarily mean easy to understand. Simple means there are no hidden or double meanings. Simple is saying what you mean. As Albert Day said, "Where there's simplicity words can be taken at face value. One says what one means and means what one says."

Simplicity means there's no "joker" hiding in the language to nullify its obvious intent.

Both Jesus and Paul were characterized by simplicity. Their intention was not to confuse or deceive but to clarify and illuminate. Paul was not always easy to understand, nor was Jesus. Where there's simplicity there is no artificiality. One does not try to appear younger or wiser or richer than one is. Or more saintly. Moffatt's translation of 1 Cor. 13:4 hits it exactly when it says, "Love makes no parade, gives itself no airs."

Answer to the egg problem: Drop the egg from a height of four feet.

This problem points out our tendency to misunderstand the goal of the solution. You may have assumed that the goal was not to break the egg, when the problem was only how to get the egg to drop three feet without breaking.

8

Look for the Second Right Answer

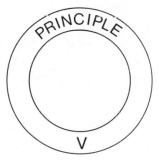

Nothing is more dangerous than an idea when it is the only one we have.

Emile Chartier

If I ran a school, I'd give the average grade to the one who gave me all the right answers, for being good parrots. I'd give the top grades to those who made a lot of mistakes and told me about them, and then told me what they learned from them.

Buckminster Fuller

Children are perhaps the most creative among us because as someone said, "they are fresh from God." They have a natural sense of curiosity and creativity, of wonder and connection with the world. Unfortunately, our educational process often curbs this inborn curiosity by intimating that there is only one right answer to questions. Children get "credit" for the one right answer, the only one they can give and still be considered "good students." As a result they begin to limit their vision, fearing the potential wrongness of other answers. We have taught them to stifle one of God's greatest gifts—creativity.

Creativity is being able to look at whatever else people are looking at—and think something totally different. It's the ability to rearrange old patterns into new ones, to combine two ideas in a way that no one has ever done before. If we are to combine ideas into original ways of thinking, we need to have more than one idea—but we have been taught to look for only one right answer.

Reality, however, doesn't always cooperate with our ways of thinking; life rarely present us with only one option, with only one solution to a problem. Life is more ambiguous than that, and in fact, there are many right answers—all depending on what you are looking for.

Roger Von Oech believes that problems are simply "a whack on the side of the head," an abrupt interruption, sometimes from God Himself, that causes us to think about life differently and perhaps even take a different route in our lives.

Von Oech observes that people try to avoid problems by acting on their first impulse rather than by trying to discover alternate solutions. There are several dangers to this impulsive method of problem solving.

First, acting on the first right answer limits us to one course of action while discovering other possible solutions creates multiple possibilities and increases flexibility.

Second, an idea or a solution is best understood in the context of other ideas. If we have only one idea, we can't compare it to anything else, so we don't know its strengths and weaknesses. In this way, ideas are like musical notes, which have meaning only in relationship to other notes.

Looking for the second right answer is not only an important survival technique, it can also be a great deal of fun. Consider, for example, the following problem. When you come up with an answer, deliberately change your point of view and come up with another answer. After you do that, look for the third right answer. In truth, there are many.

• Add one line to the Roman numeral eleven and end up with the number ten.

XI

Now think of two other ways to do it.

While you're puzzling over it, let me relate a story from Alexander Caladera that certainly demonstrates the principle of finding the second right answer.

He received a call from a colleague who asked if he would be the referee on the grading of an examination question. The professor was about to give a student a zero for his answer to a physics question, while the student claimed he should receive a perfect score and would if the system were not set up against the student. The instructor and the student agreed to submit this to an impartial arbiter, and Caladera was selected.

He went to his colleague's office and read the examination question: "Show how it is possible to determine the height of a tall building with the aid of a barometer."

The student had answered, "Take the barometer to the top of the building, attach a long rope to it, lower the barometer to the street, and then bring it up, measuring the length of the rope. The length of the rope is the height of the building."

Caladera pointed out that the student really had a strong case for full credit, since he had answered the question completely and correctly. On the other hand, if full credit were given, it could well contribute to a high grade for the student in his physics class. A high grade is supposed to certify competence in physics, but the answer did not confirm this. He suggested that the student have another try at answering the question. Caladera was not surprised that his colleague agreed, but he was surprised that the student did.

He gave the student six minutes to answer the question, with the warning that his answer should show some knowledge of physics. At the end of five minutes he had not written anything. Caladera asked if he wished to give up, but he said no. He had many answers to this problem; he was just thinking of the best one. In the next minute, he dashed off his answer which read:

"Take the barometer to the top of the building and lean over the edge of the roof. Drop the barometer, timing its fall with a stopwatch. Then, using the formula $S = \frac{1}{2}at^2$, calculate the height of the building."

At this point, Caladera asked his colleague if he would give up. He conceded and gave the student almost full credit.

In leaving the office, he recalled that the student had said he had other answers to the problem, so he asked him what they were.

"Oh yes," said the student, "there are many ways of getting the height of a tall building with the aid of a barometer. For example, you could take the barometer out on a sunny day and measure the height of the barometer, the length of its shadow, and the length of the shadow of the building, and by the use of a simple proportion, determine the height of the building.

"There is a very basic measurement method that you will like. In this method, you take the barometer and begin to walk up the stairs. As you climb the stairs, you mark off the length of the barometer along the wall. You then count the number of marks and this will give you the height of the building in barometer units. A very direct method. Of course, if you want a more sophisticated method, you can tie the barometer to the end of a string, swing it as a pendulum, and determine the value of 'g' at the street level and at the top of the building. From the difference between the two values of 'g', the height of the building can, in principle, be calculated.

"Finally," he concluded, "there are many other ways of solving the problem. Probably the best is to take the barometer to the basement and knock on the superintendent's door. When the superintendent answers, you say: 'Mr. Superintendent, here I have a fine, rather expensive barometer. If you will tell me the height of this building, I will give it to you.'"

At this point, Caladera asked the student if he really did not know the conventional answer to this question. He admitted he did, but said that he was fed up with high school and college instructors trying to teach him what to think rather than how to think, to explore the deep inner logic of the subject in a pedantic way, as is often done in the new mathematics, rather than teaching him the genuine structure of the subject.

Now let's return to our problem with the Roman numeral eleven. The most obvious solution is to add a fraction bar.

$$X/I$$

Ten divided by one is ten

Other solutions could include crossing the one:

$$X \mathbf{\dagger}$$

Ten plus nothing is ten

or drawing a horizontal line through the figure

$$\cancel{XI}$$

This makes VI and IV (upside down), together they make ten

or drawing a horizontal line beside the figure

$$XI-$$

When this is turned sideways it becomes X/I, which is ten

The solutions shown above are just some of those that involve the use of a straight line. However, the problem statement was: "add one line . . ." with no qualifications as to the shape of the line, it would be an unwarranted assumption to try to solve this problem with only straight lines.

As long as we produce a mark with just one sweep of the pen, without lifting the pen from the paper, it produces one line. With this in mind, the following solutions are permissible:

$$XI\hspace{-0.4em}\text{—}$$

A proofreader's deletion mark

$$X\sqrt{I}$$

Ten times the square root of one is ten

$$\textit{ten}\,XI$$

Ten times one is ten

Or Rick Vander Kam offered this as another right solution,

$$X \cdot I$$

A dot between numerals like this indicates that you are multiplying, hence, ten times one is ten

What practical application can this exercise have to our lives? Many of the best things that have ever happened to me have stemmed from my coming up with the second right answer. When I finished my studies at Stanford, I had several options of what to do with my life.

My first choice was to apply for a job as the head coach for the freshman football team at Stanford. After much thinking, my second choice was to accept a job as San Francisco Bay area director for Young Life. As it worked out, there were forty-nine applicants for the coaching job. It finally narrowed down to two, me and Dick Vermeil. Yes, *the* Dick Vermeil. At that time he had coached for many years, and later he went on to be the head coach at Stanford, then at UCLA, and finally with the NFL Philadelphia Eagles.

Obviously, I was not chosen that year. So I took my second choice working with Young Life—and it ended up changing my life forever in some powerful and unexpected ways.

In fact, one year later when they moved Vermeil up to a varsity coaching position, I was offered the job as the head freshman coach at Stanford. By then I was so excited about working with these crazy high school kids for $200 a month that I turned down a $20,000 coaching job. I believe that has been one of the more significant decisions in my lifetime.

In writing some notes in my journal recently, I realized that much of my life has been based on second choices—and second chances. Writing, in fact for me, was not my first choice, and yet it is where I now have the opportunity to "taste life twice."

Similarly, seminar and conference speaking was another *second* choice that God is now using in ways that I never would have imagined. Likewise, when I was younger I was very committed to developing *my* leadership skills, but God has led me to a second choice of exploring His concept of *servant* leadership, which I intend to develop for the rest of my life.

Very few people know that Henry Ford did *not* plan to go into the automobile business, but rather into the locomotive business. His first creative exploit as a youth on his father's farm was to build a steam engine. His life's aim was to make railroad equipment. Not until he was nearly forty years old did he set his goal on making passenger cars.

After college, I realized that my second choice was really the result of God's leading. Then the following Sunday I had this decision confirmed in a great way when in church the pastor gave a sermon called "Paul's Second Choice." It was based on Acts 16:6-10 where Paul wanted to go to Phrygia and Galatia, but the Holy Spirit prevented them from speaking God's message in Asia. As it says there, "When they came to Mysia they tried to enter Bithynia, but again the Spirit of Jesus would not allow them. So they passed by Mysia and came down to Troas, where one night Paul had a vision of a Macedonian man standing and appealing to him in the words: 'Come over to Macedonia and help us!'" (Acts 16:7-9, PHILLIPS). From this point on, Paul made every effort to go to Macedonia (his second choice), and through that God brought the message of the gospel to the whole world.

Look for the second right answer, the third right answer, and maybe even the fourth. Then compare them and choose what is truly the best option for your problem and your life. Who knows, like Paul, it may change your life.

Here are a couple helpful hints for finding the second right answer. Change the way you ask questions. Play with your wording of the question to get different answers. Solicit plural answers, for example, instead of singular answers. Instead of phrasing the question so that people look for "the" right answer, train yourself to ask "what are the answers" or "what are the results that you are looking for." Often the really creative idea is just outside your reach, but with a little more effort and creativity, you'll come to an answer that will truly satisfy your problem.

9

Ask Dumb Questions

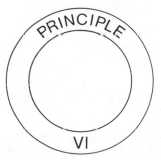

Judge a man by his questions rather than by his answers.

Voltaire

The silly question is the first intimation of some totally new development.

Alfred North Whitehead

There aren't any embarrassing questions—just embarrassing answers.

Carl Rowan

It is better to ask some of the questions than to know all of the answers.

James Thurber

Problem solving is basically a process of asking questions. The tougher the problem, the better the questions must be. In reality there is no such thing as a dumb question. In fact, sometimes the simplest and most obvious questions (those that seem dumb) are often the most profound.

Tom Peters, in his bestselling *Thriving on Chaos*, says, "You must have the guts to ask dumb questions. I was blessed early in my consulting career. . . . My first boss. . . . was smart enough and comfortable enough with himself to ask really elementary (some would say dumb) questions. Mostly it's the "dumb," elementary questions followed by a dozen even more elementary questions that will yield pay dirt."

Mark Twain once said, "We are all ignorant—but just in different areas." Perhaps it is the beginning of wisdom never to pretend that you know something when you don't. An ancient proverb says, "Ask a dumb question and be embarrassed for a moment; don't ask it and be embarrassed for a lifetime."

The key to problem solving is not to look for answers but for quality questions. We are all given six powerful tools: what, why, where, when, how, and who. How well we employ them will make a distinct difference in our problem-solving abilities. Consider the following diagram. What is the next pattern in the sequence?

What should the next character in the pattern look like? In approaching any kind of problem we need to look at it from as many different angles as possible: sideways, backwards, from the top, from the bottom. You may look at this and ask yourself "how does it look upside-down?" Or do you see anything new in reading it backward? Or turn it on end, does a vertical arrangement give you any clues? Or look at it in a mirror.

Perhaps you should ask yourself what category this problem fits in. Is it a geometry problem? A word problem? Is there symbolism involved? Is it a math problem? Do parts of it look like things you've seen before? For example, the second pattern looks like a heart, therefore could it relate to the suit symbols in cards? Or the last symbol looks something like an upside-down female symbol but then where would the male symbol be? What things repeat themselves or seem strange (i.e., why do some have horizontal bars and some not? And why are they at different levels?)?

Questions are such a potent tool in creative problem solving. Does the problem have any symmetry? As a whole? Or horizontal symmetry? Or vertical symmetry? (Yes, in fact, in each character.)

Aha! Now we're getting somewhere. Look at the left half of each character, then look at the right half of each character (bingo!). Can you see in the symmetry that each one is a number mirrored symmetrically. Look carefully, and you'll notice that the first pattern is a one with a one mirrored back symmetrically. The second pattern is a two with a symmetrical back. Hence, a three, a four, a five, and so the next characters would look like this.

Asking questions is vital, as three ancient proverbs suggest.

He who would asks questions cannot avoid the answers.
Cameroonian proverb

Better ask twice than lose your way once.
Danish proverb

To question a wise man is the beginning of wisdom.
German proverb

Children are natural question askers, radiating curiosity. It has been said that 90 percent of all children are creative, but by the age of sixteen that number drops to 40 percent; by the age of fifty-six less than 2 percent of the population is considered creative.

Ray Rood, one of the premier thinkers in child developmental studies, said, "Four-year-olds are perhaps the greatest geniuses in our society; they are at the quintessence of their creativity. Then they enter school." Perhaps we lose touch with these creative abilities because we cease asking questions. Perhaps we don't ask more questions because we think our questions are dumb. Our ego gets in the way. We are afraid of making mistakes. We are afraid of being seen as a fool, or of being criticized. We are afraid to ask questions about something we're supposed to know.

All of the great inventions and discoveries occurred because people asked questions, sometimes dumb questions. Because we live in an answer-oriented society, people usually ask what is the answer, instead of what is the next question.

Roger Von Oeck tells a story about the automotive genius Charles Kettering that exemplifies the importance of asking questions.

In 1912 Charles Kettering became interested in solving the problem of gasoline "knock"—gasoline burning too slowly in the cylinder—in order to improve fuel efficiency. Kettering began to ask questions. He was primarily concerned with causing the gasoline to combust earlier in the cylinder. He began to focus on the word "early." So he thought about those things that happened "early," including historical, physical, and biological models.

He studied a particular plant, the trailing arbutus, which blooms early. Since its distinctive feature was its red leaves, Kettering assumed that the red color that enabled the plant to retain certain wavelengths of light also made the plant bloom early. He began to ask a new series of questions, "How can I make the gasoline red?" "If I put red dye in gasoline, will it combust earlier?"

Unfortunately—or fortunately—Kettering had no red dye in his workshop, but he did have some iodine. When he added iodine to gasoline, the engine didn't knock. Feeling a little uncertain about using iodine, Kettering repeated the experiment several days later, after he had acquired some red dye. This time the engine knocked.

Kettering came to understand that the "red" color didn't eliminate the 'knock,' but something in the iodine did. His questions then focused on the additives in iodine, and he subsequently solved his problem of engine knock. Had he not begun with simple questions he might not have discovered the solution.[1]

---

[1] Roger Von Oech, *A Whack in the Side of the Head* (New York: Warner Books, 1983), 90–91.

Einstein said that imagination is more important than knowledge. Our imagination is best expressed by the quality, the boldness, and the sometimes the unpredictability and innovativeness of our questions.

- What is the nicest compliment you've ever received?
- If you could describe your life in five words, what would they be?
- What are three things that always bring a smile to your face?
- What three things frustrate you most?
- If you could change two things about your life, what would they be?
- What are two things you want from God?
- What are two things you think God wants from you?

There is absolutely no limit to our creativity when it comes to asking questions. But most importantly we must be willing (in fact eager) to ask "dumb" questions.

Suppose I give you the following series of numbers: 1, 4, 9, 16, 25, 36, 49. You would likely recognize a pattern here and realize that each of the numbers is the square of its position in that series. So that you would probably predict the next number in the series would be 64.

Now what if you saw this list:

painted eggs
pranks
fireworks
John Philip Sousa music
champagne
shamrocks
candy canes
jack-o'-lanterns

What kind of questions do you need to ask in order to solve a pattern like this? What's the similarity between the painted eggs and fireworks? What do pranks and jack-o'-lanterns have in common? What images do you get from each of these statements? Questions stretch your thinking, making it more effective. Questions stimulate associations and connections you wouldn't possible notice otherwise.

Perhaps after reading this list you realize that all these things are associated with American holidays. And if we continued this list you wouldn't be surprised to find eggnog, heart-shaped candy, potato salad, tinsel, ground hogs, and cherry trees.[2]

On her deathbed, Gertrude Stein is said to have been asked, "What is the answer?" Then after a long silence, she said, "What is the question?"

The Bible could be looked at as a Book of questions. In fact, Frederick Buechner says in *Wishful Thinking*, "Don't start looking in the Bible for the answers it gives, start by listening to the questions it asks. There is perhaps no stronger reason for reading the Bible than that somewhere among all those India paper pages there awaits each reader, whoever he is, at least one question which for years he may have been pretending not to hear. It could be a central question of his own life."

Here are a few of those central questions. Notice that these are simple but very profound.

- What is a man profited, if he shall gain the whole world, and lose his own soul? (Matt. 16:26)
- Am I my brother's keeper? (Gen. 4:9)
- If God be for us, who can be against us? (Rom. 8:31)
- What is truth? (John 18:38)
- How can a man be born when he is old? (John 3:4)
- What profit hath a man of all his labor which he taketh under the sun? (Eccles. 1:3)
- Whither shall I go from thy Spirit? (Ps. 139:7)
- Who is my neighbor? (Luke 10:29)
- What shall I do to inherit eternal life? (Luke 10:25)

Simple questions, profound questions. The Bible is essentially a Book in which God asks man many questions, and man in turn asks God many questions. But the answers depend on the questions.

---

[2] Ibid., 45.

Take a chance. Next time you are inclined to ask, ask. Keep a list of the best questions you've ever heard. Practice the art of asking good questions. Learn how to design questions so that they will penetrate beyond the surface, so that they will elicit a maximum amount of information. Learn how to frame questions so that you can see both what the real problem is and then what the best solutions are. Let the childlike curiosity in you grow. And don't forget that oftentimes the best questions are the "dumb" ones, the simplest and the most obvious.

Albert Schweitzer said, "For us the great men are not those who solved the problems, but those who *discovered* them."

10

Unlock Your Creativity

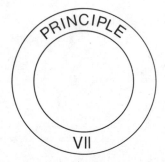

After all, if you are living a hum-drum life, and you do nothing to change it, ten years from now you will be a product of ten more years of hum-drumidness.

David Campbell

Millions long for immortality, and yet don't know what to do on a rainy Sunday afternoon.

Susan Ertz

Everyone is born a genius, but the process of living de-geniuses them.

Buckminster Fuller

The Lord gave you two ends, one for sitting and one for thinking. Your success depends upon which you use. Heads you win; tails you lose.

Creativity is a gift from God, and no one is excluded from receiving this gift. All people are creative in one way or another. Recognize and accept that you are probably far more creative than you realize. Do you know in which area you are creative?

There are two primary reasons why most of us are not more creative than we presently are. First, much of what we do does not demand a high level of creativity. Routine is an energy-saving device. Many of us drive to work the same way every day and handle many matters of daily living in a rather routine, constant way.

However, we must realize that our future is not going to be more of the same routine. Change will be the norm in the ever-increasingly complex future that faces all of us. We will no longer be able to solve today's and tomorrow's problems with yesterday's solutions. Nevertheless, we have a choice. We can either spend our time and energy complaining about how things aren't as easy as they used to be or we can begin to employ and develop some of our God-given creative abilities and thus discover new ideas, new answers, and new solutions. As someone once said, "If you do what you've always done and think what you've always thought, there's a good chance you'll get what you've always got."

Second, many of us are not more creative because we don't think of ourselves as being creative. As I pointed out earlier, the only scientifically distinguishable difference between creative and noncreative people is that creative people *think* they are creative and noncreative people think they are *not* creative. An I'm-not-creative attitude is a self-fulfilling prophecy.

So, if you want to be more creative, begin by thinking of yourself as being more creative. *Practice* being creative. Creativity isn't just for those few in the arts or sciences or those who patent new inventions or new theories. It's a vital necessity for our everyday living. You can employ creativity in your home or your workplace, in your profession or your hobbies, in raising your children or in keeping the romance alive in your marriage. The possibilities are endless. If you want to feel creative, act creative. The unforgivable sin of problem solving may be having a mind that's "made up."

Alan Alda is right when he says, "Be brave enough to live creatively. The creative is the place where no one else has ever been. You have to leave the city of your comfort and go into the wilderness of your intuition. You can't get there by bus, but only by hard work and risk. And by not quite knowing what you are doing. What you'll discover will be wonderful; what you'll discover will be yourself."

Dr. Gregory Zilborg says, "An artist who knows exactly what he is doing, in absolute detail, is a dead technician."

There's no one right way to be creative just as there are no single right ways to solve problems. Each person has his or her own way to be creative as this ad promoting National Library Week reveals:

abcdefghijklmnopqrstuvwxyz

At your public library they've got these two dozen and two little rivets of ink arranged in ways that can make you cry, giggle, love, hate, wonder, ponder, and understand. Each is shaped—of straight lines and curved—to stimulate almost infinite varieties of thought.

It's astonishing what those twenty-six little letters can do.

In Shakespeare's hands they become *Hamlet*. Mark Twain wound them into *Huckleberry Finn*. James Joyce twisted them into *Ulysses*. Gibbon pondered them in *The Decline and Fall of the Roman Empire*. Milton shaped them into *Paradise Lost*. Einstein added some numbers and signs (to save time and space) and they formed the general theory of relativity . . .

Being creative means taking everyday material—like the alphabet—and turning it into something extraordinary. Each of us is unique, formed in the image of the Creator. That means that each of us has the gift of creativity, but to fully explore our creativity takes commitment, hard work, and enthusiasm. Interestingly, the word "enthusiasm" comes from a Greek root meaning "God within you." Therefore since God is within us, we all have sufficient enthusiasm to complete any project—all we have to do is express that enthusiasm.

"God was here, but I was not aware of Him." How many times does Scripture (and modern life) reflect this theme? Light filters through the window from its source some 93 million miles away.

We are surrounded by the many miracles of life, and yet we fail to recognize them. Our world is as vast as our imaginations—or as small. The choice is ours.

We are all endowed with the remarkable, absolutely phenomenal 17-percent water-based, analog, electrochemical, digital, quintrasensing, servomechanism computer, otherwise known as a brain, that can do absolutely astonishing things. Like any gift we've been given we must use it; we must exercise it in order to grow. This is critical, for our creativity will atrophy if unused. Creativity doesn't take genius as much as it takes exercise. Teddy Roosevelt said, "Do what you can, with what you have, where you are."

You can start to unlock your creativity through the following exercise. The first ten letters of the alphabet are divided into two groups, indented below:

Group 1 is: A E F H I
Group 2 is: B C D G J

What is the pattern that differentiates the two groups? If you can recognize it, which group would you put capital K into? How about capital R? Or capital T? THIMBK! What are the similarities? What are the differences? Is there something distinctly different about the shapes between group 1 and group 2? You might notice that the letters in group 1 have only straight lines, while the letters in group 2 have both straight and curved lines. Thus, capital K and capital T would fit into group number 1, while capital R belongs in group number 2.[1]

Creativity well may be the most important survival skill we have as we face an incredibly complex future. If we are to solve some of the problems of hunger, loneliness, war, stress, and boredom it will take more than a little bit of creativity. All of us are blessed with the gift of creativity, but we do need to stretch it and use it. Said Carl Jung, "If you have nothing at all to create, then perhaps you should create yourself."

---

[1] Roger Von Oech, *A Kick in the Seat of the Pants* (New York: Harper & Row, 1986), 34.

Each of us is called to be the expert on our own lives. Find a new hobby. Take a course at a local junior college. Write a short story. See a play. Take up a musical instrument. Record your ideas in a journal for the next six months. Or, read a good book on creativity. Two of the best are by Roger Von Oech—*A Whack on the Side of the Head* and *A Kick in the Seat of the Pants*. Or, you could read David Campbell's *Take the Road to Creativity—And Get off Your Dead End*.

Most moms are exceptionally creative although they don't realize it. Many dads employ creativity daily at their workplace but don't realize how they could enhance it. Most students fail to exercise the full gifts of creativity in the classroom. Alex Osborne, one of the founding fathers of Brainstorming and Creative Problem Solving, once said, "Creativity is so delicate a flower that praise tends to make it bloom, while discouragement often nips it in the bud. Any of us will put out more and better ideas if our efforts are truly appreciated."

Encourage creativity in each other and in your children. David Campbell tells the story about a ten-year-old neighbor:

Some friends came home with us one night for a visit. I filled some glasses with ice from the refrigerator and poured us all a soft drink. As we sat there talking and sipping, I thought that mine tasted strange, a bit salty. I ignored it, but the salt taste got stronger. Then one of my friends said, "What did you put in my soda, sea water? It tastes funny."

I said, "So does mine. I don't know what happened—let me get you another." So I fixed everyone a new glass, but in a few minutes we all had the same problem; the drink still tasted salty.

"I'm not sure we would have ever figured out the trouble if Sandy, our ten-year-old, hadn't come in just then, opened the refrigerator door, and asked, "Who took my ice cubes?"

So the story came out. "My teacher said that salt water wouldn't freeze, so I was trying it out. I put different amounts of salt in several ice cube trays to see what would happen. What did you do with all the trays?"[2]

---

[2] David Campbell, *Take the Road to Creativity—And Get Off Your Dead End* (Valencia, Calif.: Argus Communications, 1985), 66–67.

Fortunately these parents were proud of their child's curiosity and took the episode in stride. The moral of the story is, if you are going to encourage creativity around the house, you might occasionally expect a few salty ice cubes.

• Here are a few more puzzles to stretch your creativity. By moving one—and only one—line, make this into a correct equation.

$$IV = III + III$$

Try to solve it before you look below. The answer to this first puzzle is a simple one:

$$VI = III + III$$

The only difficulty is remembering your Roman numerals well enough to know that $IV = 4$ and $VI = 6$. The second puzzle is slightly harder:

$$VII + V = I$$

There are at least two possible answers. Try to find both before reading any further. Possible answers to the second puzzle are:

$$VII - VI = I \text{ or } VII - V = II$$

This puzzle is more complicated than the first one because you have to do more than just tinker with numbers; you must change an algebraic sign. You have to steer away from straight-ahead thinking to consider other possibilities.

The third puzzle (same rule) is:

$$II = VI$$

Don't look at the answer below until you've tried to solve it. One solution is:

$$I = V\overline{I}$$

This solution is complicated because it requires the use of the square root symbol ($\sqrt{\ }$). The flexibility afforded by lines for symbols as well as numbers is still required, and to that is added the need for mathematical sophistication, namely, an ability to work with a square root.

Creativity isn't just for the selected few. Since there is nothing new under the sun, it means simply putting old things together in a new and a fresh way. Creativity is especially expressed in the ability to make connections, to make associations, to turn things around and express them in a new way.

As an exaggerated illustration of why laws of association cannot be pinned down, Alex Osborne said that there's a weird passage his daughter loved to quote while at college:

What is a double petunia? A petunia is a flower like a begonia. A begonia is a meat like a sausage. A sausage and battery is a crime. Monkeys crime trees. Tree's a crowd. A crow crowd in the morning and made a noise. A noise is on your face between your eyes. Eyes are opposite from nays. A colt nays. You go to bed with a colt, and wake up in the morning with a case of double petunia.

11

Scratch Where It Itches

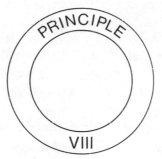

A good problem statement often includes:

   (a) what is known;
   (b) what is unknown; and
   (c) what is sought

Edward Hodnett

Troubles you see . . . is the generalization word for what
God exists in . . . the thing is not to get hung up.

Jack Kerouac

Life is often ambiguous and untidy. There are always loose ends.
It is sticky, hot, cold, lukewarm at times—and frequently messy
and unmanageable. Most of life is somewhere in between, in the

middle—amidst small frustrations and a lot of "I don't know what to do next." Most of life is not elegant or sophisticated.

We get stuck in habits, and everything seems to be moving and changing faster than we can keep it in repair. The mystery runs dry. And more often than not, our feeling about this escalation of problems of our times borders on insecurity.

All forecasts for the upcoming year point to a period of unprecedented change. To cope with these problems and pressures, we must become active participants in the change process. We must face reality squarely and assume the responsibility for ordering our lives. We must also know what problems to solve and what to avoid—focusing clearly on the problems that are ours.

It is extremely important that we do not run away from discomfort—but at the same time we should not invite or provoke unnecessary problems. Life is complicated and difficult enough—we should not grab all the free-floating guilt and take it upon ourselves. We tend to adopt problems which aren't really ours. We tend to grease wheels that aren't really squeaking. Our lives become cluttered with problems that don't belong to us.

In this section, I want to focus primarily on four things:

1. Don't fix it if it ain't broke
2. Don't rework or rehash problems that are already solved
3. Don't "own" problems that are not your responsibility
4. Focus on what the problem really is

DON'T FIX IT IF IT AIN'T BROKE

There are three situations when we try to fix something that isn't broken. The first is the result of assuming that someone with a problem wants, or needs, for us to provide a solution. As I pointed out earlier, many people just want you to listen sympathetically. They're not asking for a solution, just an attentive ear.

The second situation occurs when we spend valuable energy solving problems that don't exist. When we don't have all the facts, our fears, suspicions, assumptions, or expectations lead us to anticipate problems that don't exist. Those of us who like to control things anticipate problems that never occur, and at times when we are in an emotional havoc, we latch onto problems that would not otherwise be there.

The third situation is a byproduct of emotional stress. When we're emotionally distraught, we often cannot distinguish our original problem from those caused by our emotional distress.

DON'T REHASH SOLVED PROBLEMS

Have you ever had that feeling where you say, "What am I doing here again? Haven't I been here before?" Sometimes this occurs when we are so emotionally attached to a problem that we refuse to let it go even after its been solved (or apparently solved). Thomas Edison said, "It takes about seven years to convert the average man to the acceptance of a solved problem."

Yet when we've solved a problem, we need to have the good sense to realize it has been solved. If we still hang onto something long after it has been taken care of, we need to ask some "What and why?" questions:

- What am I hanging onto?
- Why am I hanging onto it?
- What's really the issue here?
- What am I hiding?
- What keeps me from being more detached in this situation?
- What keeps me from releasing this problem to the past?
- What past emotional issues keep clouding today's problems?
- Are there perhaps some unresolved issues (which could be in-law issues, children issues, relationship issues, money issues, etc.) that keep surfacing in current problems?

DON'T "OWN" OTHER PEOPLE'S PROBLEMS

One of the foundational principles in Thomas Gordon's Parent Effectiveness Training (PET) is problem ownership. Many parents fall into the trap of assuming responsibility for problems that really belong to their children. Children should solve their problems themselves.

Sadly, if we do not allow our children to assume responsibility for their own problems, we communicate to them that they cannot be trusted with solving their own problems. Such a message haunts both child and parents for decades.

PET advocates active listening (i.e., giving feedback so that the person feels that he or she is being heard) as an excellent tool for communicating acceptance of a person with a problem. PET strongly encourages you to remember that other persons, including your own child, are people separate from you, capable of talking about and finding their own solutions to problems.[1]

If you try to solve the problems of others you need to ask yourself questions such as these:

- What's it going to take for me to let that person solve his or her own problem?
- What keeps me from letting them solve it?
- What is it that makes my investment in how it's solved so high?
- Who's wearing the hat in this one?
- Why am I taking this problem away from my child, spouse, friend?

I highly recommend to you Carmen Renee Berry's *When Helping You Is Hurting Me, Escaping the Messiah Trap* to help you recognize who "owns" the problem. She defines the "messiah trap" as a deadly lie because it encourages behavior that appears noble, godly, and gracious. Yet the messiah trap has two faces. One convinces us, "If you don't do it, it won't get done." Those who believe they must help others are most vulnerable to this. A person with a messiah complex feels he or she is responsible for making sure that everything turns out all right and that everybody is happy, but "messiahs" can hurt others by trying to help them. Their actions (and assumptions) can block honest communication, encourage feelings of helplessness and inadequacy in others, make people angry, control and manipulate others, and interfere with growth by withholding information or breaking confidentiality.

---

[1] To learn more about Parent Effectiveness Training, I recommend you read Thomas Gordon, *P.E.T. in Action* (New York: Bantam Books, 1976).

The other side of the messiah trap makes one believe that everyone else's needs take priority over his or hers. That makes it terribly difficult to care for one's own legitimate needs. Attempted self-nurturing is seen as selfish, and, for such a person, being selfish is viewed as the worst of all sins.

WHAT REALLY IS THE PROBLEM?

This is one of the core issues of this book, and, therefore, it cannot be emphasized enough. Before you can solve a problem, it is critical that you understand what the problem really is.

It is often said that a problem well-defined is half solved. Roger Von Oech's *A Kick in the Seat of the Pants* includes Tom Hirshfield's rules of thumb, which are good suggestions in helping you scratch where it itches. He says:

- Never state a problem to yourself in the same terms as it was brought to you.
- The second assault on the same problem should come from a totally different direction.
- If you don't understand a problem, then explain it to someone else and listen to yourself.
- Don't mind approaches that transform one problem into another. That's a new chance.
- If it's surprising, it's useful.
- Studying the inverse problem always helps.

Don't waste time scratching where it doesn't itch. What is the priority in this problem? What are the core issues? What is the central focus?

We need to concentrate on the essentials, eliminating everything that is unnecessary. For example, you might ask yourself what *isn't* the problem? What can I exclude, eliminate, delete, or forget? You might even ask, "What am I avoiding?" It is critical to isolate your problem, to separate it, to untangle it from other problems and issues so that you are working with a clear focus.

Look at the problem rather than at its symptoms. A symptom, like a fever, often attracts our attention first, but fever is usually not the problem. It is only a symptom of a larger problem. Soothing a fever will not cure malaria, the flu, or some other serious ailment. Have you ever heard anyone say: "If I just got rid of my husband, my job, my employee, my _____, my _____, then everything would be OK." Changing spouses, jobs, friends, employees, or whatever is often only a classic case of treating the symptom instead of the illness.

Simply stated, you can't cure a problem until you know what that problem really is. In many instances, when you see the problem clearly you'll also be able to see the solution. Likewise, many of our problems—too many—are greatly amplified because of the lack of proper communication.

I once heard a speaker suggest three things for problem solving:

- Number 1, define your problem carefully.
- Number 2, redefine your problem carefully.
- Number 3, re-redefine your problem carefully.

The following story is well known, but it illustrates what can happen when we fail to define our problems properly:

An English woman looking for a room in Switzerland asked the schoolmaster of the village where she wanted to live to help her. After finding a place that suited her, she returned to London for her baggage. Once there, however, she remembered that she hadn't asked about a bathroom, or "water closet," as she called it. So she wrote the village schoolmaster with her question, referring to these facilities in her letter as a "WC."

The schoolmaster, puzzled by these initials, sought the help of a parish priest. The priest decided the woman must be asking about a wayside chapel.

You can imagine the woman's confusion when she received the following letter from the schoolmaster:

Dear Madam:

I regret very much the delay in answering your letter. But I now take the pleasure in informing you that a "WC" is located about 9 miles from the house, in the center of a beautiful grove of trees. It is capable of seating 250 people at a time. It is open Tuesday, Thursday, and Sunday each week. I admit it is quite a distance away if you are in the habit of going regularly, but no doubt you will be pleased to know that a great number of people take their lunches along and make a day of it. They usually arrive early and stay late.

The last time my wife and I went was six years ago. It was so crowded we had to stand the whole time we were there. It may interest you to know that there is a supper being planned to raise money to buy more seats. Likewise, it may interest you to know that my daughter met her husband the first time in the "WC," and they were later married in the "WC."

I would like to say it pains me very much not to be able to go more regularly, but it is surely no lack of desire on my part. As we grow older, it seems to be more of an effort, particularly in cold weather. If you should decide to come for a visit, perhaps I could go with you the first time you go, sit with you, and introduce you to all the other folks. Remember, this is a friendly community.

Yours truly
The Schoolmaster

12

Make It Fun

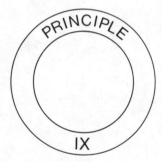

If you could choose one characteristic that would get you through life, choose a sense of humor.

Jennifer Jones

High heels were invented by somebody who was kissed on the forehead.

Christopher Morley

When a man sits with a pretty girl for an hour, it seems like a minute. But let him sit on a hot stove for a minute, and it's longer than an hour. That's relativity.

Albert Einstein

If lawyers are disbarred and clergymen defrocked, doesn't it follow that electricians can be delighted; musicians denoted; cowboys deranged; tree surgeons debarked; and dry cleaners depressed?

Virginia Ostman

Of all the things God created, I am often most grateful he created laughter.

Charles Swindoll

One day I was meeting the president of our board for lunch at the Bonaventure Hotel in downtown Los Angeles. Dressed in a three-piece business suit, I was attempting to appear dignified when an incident occurred which I still slightly blame on the waitress. If she had just seated us immediately, it never would have happened. She walked off, however, and left us standing there for five or ten minutes. Given that amount of time, my devious mind can often figure out some way to have fun.

In front of the dining room stood a huge sign that read: "Please wait to be seated." Signs such as this are seldom as elegant as this one. It was made of brass, framed, and was absolutely stunning. As I studied this sign more closely, I realized that the restrooms were right next to us. So I did what I thought was the obvious and important thing to do; I slid the sign over in front of the restrooms—and waited.

A few moments later an elderly couple walking hand-in-hand approached the restrooms. They read the sign—and then waited. I wondered what images must have been going through their minds. Although I thought the situation was funny, I eventually explained to them that the sign referred to the restaurant and not the restroom.

When people ask me why I do such things, I like to reply, "I can't help it: I'm a Christian." I hope that confuses people into realizing that Christians have more to celebrate than anybody in the world. Life can be fun just as problem solving can be fun, but we must make it so. Remember, as Steve Allen said, "Don't try to suppress laughter, if you do, it will go down and spread out around your hips."

Charlie Brown, the lovable cartoon character in "Peanuts," said, "I've developed a new philosophy. I only dread life one day at a time." Some people do that with problem solving; they only dread problems one at a time. Others, however, really do dread life day by day.

Yet God has given Christians a different prescription for life. Having forgiven and accepted us by His love, God wants us to have fun and enjoy life. He wants us to have a joyful spirit when we approach our problems.

God has prescribed that we live joyfully: "A cheerful heart is good medicine, but a crushed spirit dries up the bones" (Prov. 17:22, NIV). So take God's prescription for your life just as you would a doctor's. Liven up some of those dried bones and broken spirits; realize that God can and wants to generate a genuine joy within us.

Fun is not necessarily the same as joy, but fun can intensify joy. In her book, *Choosing the Amusing*, Marilyn Meberg says, "God has given to each of us an incomparable medicine bag. In it is the divinely created ability to laugh at ourselves, at our circumstances, at humor produced by others, and to take a less threatened view of everything around us. To utilize the contents of that bag is to experience healing for our minds, our souls, and our bodies."

Having fun releases our problem-solving abilities and gives us a much more objective and flexible frame of reference. It allows us to play with ideas, to use principles (such as reversal), and to expect the unexpected.

Dr. Seuss, the famous author of children's books, says, "Humor has a tremendous place in a sordid world. It's more than just a laughing matter. If you can see things out of whack, then you can certainly see how things can be in whack."

Having fun releases us from the bondage of our circumstances and gives us the capacity to laugh at our problems—and at ourselves. Having fun doesn't automatically make the pressures go away, but it helps us view them with less tension.

As Christians, we are called to reproduce the abundant life that Jesus expresses in and through us.

I was blessed to have been raised in a family where fun was valued and encouraged. When I was a senior in high school, I attended a leadership conference in eastern Washington. Like most kids my age, I always tried to be real "cool." When I dressed for bed that first night, however, I couldn't get my leg through the pajama leg opening. I kept on talking to the guy next to me, but my voice began to betray something of my predicament as I struggled to retain my cool. I then switched legs and tried to put my left foot through the left pajama leg. It, too, seemed to be folded over. Finally after some moments of frustration, I realized that my mom had sewn the pajama legs shut!

When I got home, and after a great laugh together, I warned Mom that I would get her back. Now to be good at things like this, you wait until the other person has completely forgotten the first prank. She got me in early September—I waited until Christmas.

It was to be the first time that the Ladies Home Circle ever met at our house. Our home was modest, and Mom spent weeks fixing it up and cleaning in anticipation of the meeting. As the ladies arrived, they gathered on the front porch in a semicircle, and Mom opened the door to welcome them. In the middle of her greeting she noticed that many of the ladies were peering over her shoulder and staring quizzically at the front door.

At first Mom tried to ignore this, but soon there were so many ladies staring at the front door, poking and nudging each other, that she finally had to turn around—to discover that the brand new Christmas wreath on the door was made of holly and berries and ribbons . . . and a brand new athletic supporter.

It was fun growing up in our family, and we tried to tackle problems by having fun or by making them fun as well.

Is there any way you can take any one of your problems, turn it around, and make it a little fun? Is it possible through the gift of God's grace to lighten up and even to celebrate some of the problems He has given you? Is it possible, if nothing else, to laugh at yourself? John Powell once said, "He who has learned how to laugh at himself shall never cease to be entertained."

Business executives have recently stated, "If you're not having fun, you're probably not being very productive." As I said before, we tend to enjoy doing what we do well and do well at what we enjoy. So, if you can figure out a way to enjoy the problem-solving process, you will undoubtedly be more effective.

A little boy came home and said sadly to his father, "Dad, I think I flunked my math test." The father (being a very optimistic type) said, "Son, be more positive." To which the boy replied, "Okay, Dad, I'm positive I flunked my math test."

Children have so much to teach us about spontaneity and fun. Jim, eleven years old, was doing some homework in the kitchen. His parents were sitting on the couch and smooching while watching television. Jim walked by on the way to his room, observed the scene, and casually said, "Go for it, Dad!"

Making life fun and making problem solving fun allows you to embrace change, even to love change, to enjoy it, and to get excited about the challenges that face you. A friend of mine said recently, "When anxiety attacks, if you are a believer, He can keep you from being overwhelmed." One way that God helps us not to be overwhelmed is by giving us a sense of humor.

Humorous situations are all around us if only we look for them. For example, some churches have marquees which they use to post their next Sunday's sermon title or an inviting message to passers-by. One such sign had the following invitation: "Come and Hear What Hell Is Really Like." Beneath it was the statement, "Our Choir Will Sing at Every Service."

Then there's the Texas Baptist church that printed the following in its weekly newsletter: "The ladies of the church are discarding clothing of all kinds. These ladies can be seen in the church basement between ten and twelve on Friday morning."

Victor Borge said, "Laughter is the shortest distance between two people." You can close the gap. Learn to invite joy into your life and even into your problem-solving struggles. The Scriptures remind us to delight ourselves in the Lord.

The following is a wonderful piece I received in the mail called "The Perfect Pastor."

Results of a computerized study indicate that the perfect pastor preaches exactly fifteen minutes. He condemns sin, but never upsets anyone. He works from 8:00 in the morning til 12:00 midnight and is also the janitor. He makes $60 a week, wears good clothes, buys good books, drives a good car, and gives about $50 a week to the poor. He is twenty-eight years old and has been preaching for thirty years. He is wonderfully gentle and, of course, handsome. He has a burning desire to work with teenagers and spends all his time with the senior citizens.

The perfect pastor smiles all the time with a straight face because he has a sense of humor that keeps him seriously dedicated to his work. He makes fifteen calls per day on parish families, shut-ins, and the hospitalized; he spends all his time evangelizing the unchurched, and he is always in his office when needed.

If your pastor does not measure up, simply send this letter to six other parishes that are tired of their pastor, then bundle up your pastor and send him to the church at the top of the list. In one year, you'll receive 1,643 pastors, and one of them should be perfect.

WARNING: Keep this letter going, one parish broke the chain and got its old pastor back!

JUST FOR FUN

In James Fixx's *More Games for the Super-Intelligent,* he offers this wonderfully challenging puzzle: You are a captain in charge of one sergeant and four men. Your task is to raise a 100-foot flagpole and slide it into a hole 10-feet deep. You have two ropes—one 22-feet long and one 26-feet long—two shovels, and two buckets. How do you accomplish your task? *Answer:* You turn to the sergeant and say, "Sergeant, get that flagpole up!"

Try this word game: "Woodrow Wilson's wife walked wearily through the wisteria tree because it was Woodrow's wish to whistle while he was washing the windows on the west side wall." How many "w's" are there in all? *Answer:* There are no "w's" in "all."

Here's another: Create a triangle by placing three matches adjoining each other in the form of a triangle. Can you now add three extra matches and create four equal-sided triangles? *Answer:* Create a pyramid.

Try this riddle: Which month has twenty-eight days? *Answer:* All months have twenty-eight days. Most, however, have an additional two or three days.

Here's another: It takes twelve minutes to make a hard-boiled egg. How long does it take to make twelve hard-boiled eggs? *Answer:* Twelve minutes

Here's a fun one: Bet someone that you can drop a paper match on the floor and make it land on its narrow edge every time. *Answer:* Bend the match.

And yet another: In a funny little book called *Bets You Can't Lose*,[1] one of the puzzles is to wager your adversary that he can't take his shoes and socks off by himself. *Answer:* As soon as he starts taking off his shoes, you take off yours. That way, he's not doing it by himself.

Here's one that's a little more difficult: "Glenn always has it before. Paul always takes it behind. Brian has never had it at all. Girls only have it once. Boys don't need it. Mrs. Mulligan, the widow, had it twice in succession. Dr. Lowell of Harvard had it twice as bad at the end as at the beginning." What is it? *Answer:* The letter "L."

Again, bet someone that you can stand under water for four minutes. *Answer:* Put a glass of water on your head.

And another: Challenge somebody to figure out a way to take one from twenty-nine and still have thirty left. *Answer:* Use Roman numerals (XXIX – I = XXX).

Try this one on somebody as a test of your athletic prowess. Say, "I can do twenty-five pushups with one arm. If I'm wrong, will you give me a dollar? They usually say yes. Then you refer them back to what you said, "If I'm wrong, you'll give me a dollar." You say, "Of course I'm wrong" and collect your dollar.

LAUGHTER AND FUN

Laughter and fun are the answer for everyone who wishes to lighten the load of life's burdens.

Humor can ease strain, oil relationships, reduce tensions, relieve pressures, and generally enhance the quality of life, promote confidence, and increase creativity. We all want to work with and for someone who appreciates humor and spend our lifetime in a

---

[1] Patrick B. Sullivan, *Bets You Can't Lose* (Los Angeles: Price Stern Sloan, 1979).

marriage with someone who has it. Students crave it from teachers. We appreciate it in our leaders. Politicians capitalize on it at election time. Children thrive on it when their parents and playmates constantly expose them to it. Humor liberates. It can give us the freedom to be ourselves and to take risks. It allows us to be willing to be different and to be able to make a difference.

Humor can help an individual handle discouragement, difficulty, or defeat. For example, a football coach who suffered defeat in a major game was asked when he felt the turning point occurred. He replied, "Right after the national anthem." That little bit of humor took the edge off the defeat.

Even children know the value of humor, and we're called to have a childlike heart. For example: two kids were overheard talking. One said to the other, "My dad can beat up your dad." To which the other replied, "Big deal, so can my mom!"

A story is told that somewhere in Massachusetts the people tried everything to get motorists to slow down while going through a certain residential area. They put up signs such as "Slow Down" and "Children at Play." Nothing seemed to work—until they put up a sign that said, "Nudist Colony Ahead."

Finally, here are some cute, dumb jokes my kids have brought home to me:

How can you tell a dogwood? *By its bark.*

What gets harder to catch the faster you run? *Your breath.*

What makes a terrible, loud soprano roar and charges when angry? *A bull mouse.*

What has six legs and two arms? *A sofa.*

What does it mean if you go home and you don't have to do any homework, wash your neck, or clean your room? *It means you're in the wrong house.*

As William Zinser said, "I want to make people laugh—so they will begin to see things seriously."

A FOOL AMONG HEROES

Judith Viorst wrote a catchy article for *Reader's Digest* called "The Smartest People Are Sometimes Fools," based on the maxim, "He who lives without folly is not so wise as he thinks." The article focuses on those people who are so afraid of making fools of themselves that they never take chances.

According to Viorst, fun people lacking forehand and backhand skills still go out on the tennis court. They have two left feet but still go out on the dance floor. Although they can't bend their knees or keep their skis together, they still go out on the ski slopes.

Unfortunately, in our society, those who look good seem more successful than those who have fun. In turn, we have come to value image over substance, and that is a great loss. Many are so afraid to look foolish that they refuse to take risks. Viorst, however, applauds those people who take chances, who risk failure by taking on problems and experiences that others avoid. If we do not do something simply because we fear that we might look foolish, our old age will be spent regretting our lost opportunities.

Just for the fun of it, take on a few problems that are King-Kong size, that everyone knows is impossible, that no one else will tackle. Who knows? You might surprise yourself. There's a quote that says, "We the willing, led by the unknowing, are doing the impossible for the ungrateful. We have done so much for so long for so little, we are now qualified to do anything with nothing." Take a chance.

13

Hang in There!

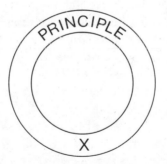

I think and think for months, for years; ninety-nine times and the conclusion is false. But the hundredth time I'm right.

Albert Einstein

I know of nothing more important than perseverance.

Genius—that power which dazzles mortal eyes, is oft but perseverance in disguise.

Henry Austin

Only he who sees the invisible can do the impossible.

It's been said in a thousand different ways. Never give up. Stick to it. Be stubborn. Persevere. Don't quit. Go the second mile. Hang in there. Invest time in your problem. It may seem like an old cliché, but it's perhaps the most important principle of all. There's no way you can get around this one. In fact, 90 percent of all failures result from people quitting too soon. If you forget everything else in this book, just remember this one principle; it could help you solve many, if not most, of your problems.

Perhaps a fresh and new way to remember it might be to simply say, "Remember Number 10" as a code phrase when you are in despair. Shout it, whisper it, mumble it, hum it, but "Remember Number 10."

In the early years of Summit Expedition, I used to go over to a pack station near where we started our courses and have a cup of coffee with Bernie Box. Bernie was a giant of a man, probably 6′ 5″ and about 275 pounds. He had an intimidating look that was intensified by a huge scar, perhaps six to eight inches long, that crossed diagonally over one eye, the result of an ax blow. Under the scar, his glass eye remained steady while his other eye moved to watch whatever he wanted to see. Although Bernie appeared to be the kind of person you thought you would not like to meet in a dark alley, in truth he was a very gentle man. He loved children, and he loved the wilderness. He loved life. I enjoyed listening to Bernie tell stories of people he had taken on pack trips. One of those stories was unforgettable.

Late one afternoon as the blue western sky was beginning to fade into oranges and grays, he got to talking about the different experiences of people on his trips who became lost in the wilderness. "I've had lots of people get lost up here," he said.

I responded, "That's probably because they don't really understand map and compass all that well. Right?"

"Nope," he said.

"Well, it's probably because they are new to the wilderness," I said.

Again he replied, "Nope."

"Then it's probably because they are city folk and don't know east from west," I said.

"Nope," he replied.

"Well, is it because they are out here for the first time and they are rookies and stuff?" I asked.

"Nope," he said.

"Then it's because they don't understand the terrain," I said.

"Nope," he said.

I must have asked him a least a dozen more questions to which I kept getting the same simple answer, "Nope." My curiosity finally won out, and I said, "Well then, how come they get lost all the time?"

"It's cause they don't go fer enuf!" he said. "I tell them to go five miles, and they go about three-fourths of a mile and start turning left and right and end up all over the place." Bernie said he spends much of his time hunting down people who are lost.

The truth of what he said hit me at more than one level. At that particular time in my life, I was somewhat lost and confused in my Christian walk. I felt that Bernie was speaking to me spiritually. I hadn't gone "fer" enough. One of the reasons we get lost in problem solving, in our relationships with one another, and in our relationship with Christ is that we don't go "fer" enough.

A famous preacher once stood up in front of more than ten thousand people at a Christian rally and said, "You're either lost or you're lost." There was a long pause in which confusion reigned, and then he repeated it again. "You're either lost or you're lost." The silence was again deafening. And he said, "You're either lost in the world or you're lost in Christ."

That evening he challenged us to understand at new levels what it means to lose your life to find it and what it means to be recklessly abandoned to the person of Jesus Christ. For something to have value, we must invest in it. Whether in our families, our relationship with Christ, or our problem-solving techniques, there's no such thing as a quick fix. There are no easy answers. As a friend of mine said, "There ain't no free lunch!" Quality living takes time and commitment. We've got to hang in there.

Tragically, we live in a society that almost forgives a person beforehand for giving up. Our culture is so focused on expediency that we often don't expect people to finish a task. Before they even begin, we forgive them for giving up. We are so committed to short-term success that we miss the importance of long-term vision.

One of the most important things I'm trying to teach my children is to finish what they start. I admire someone who stubbornly refuses to let go of a problem until it's solved.

I was probably the only person ever to attend Stanford University who had read only one book. Except for textbooks, which were required, I had read only *The Old Man and the Sea*. (I read it because it was the shortest book I could find in the library.) I was drastically unprepared for the challenges that I met at Stanford.

Only sheer endurance kept me from flunking out of college. I had to work twice as hard at my studies, but it was certainly worth it. For most of my freshman year I studied in the cafeteria at Wilbur Hall. I was such a slow reader I often didn't finish my studying until the early morning. Rather than drive ten miles back to where I lived, I'd push a table up to the cafeteria door and sleep on it, using my books for a pillow. I had to be at work there in the cafeteria at six, so when the other workers came through the door they'd knock me off the table, and I'd wake up and go to work. I convinced myself that I used sleep faster than anyone else at school. I believed that I could go to sleep at two and get up at six and still get eight hours worth of sleep. That sounds ridiculous now, but I had myself convinced, and I survived until I improved my study skills. My sleep habits improved as well.

Another person who refused to give up is Ken Taylor, the man responsible for *The Living Bible*. He started the project to provide an easy-to-understand version for his large family. While commuting to Chicago, he'd paraphrase the Scriptures into everyday language. He became so caught up in the project that he went through the entire New Testament. In his excitement over what he had produced, he sought out a publisher but was turned down. The next publisher turned him down, too. Over the months, dozens of publishers turned him down. Still determined to see his work published, Taylor used his savings to publish it himself.

During the first year, his *Living Letters* sold eight hundred copies, not very much for a book. But Ken Taylor refused to give up. Today, *The Living Bible* has sold more than 25 million copies and has been translated into countless languages. His work has touched more lives for Christ than he ever imagined possible. Ken Taylor is a walking, breathing model of perseverance!

Some years ago, I saw a film called *Why Man Creates*. Some of its scenes are still etched in my mind. I remember noting the vast amounts of time that the scientists and inventors depicted in the film invested in solving problems. One man talked excitedly about how "close" we are to solving some of the current problems with world hunger. "We've developed new strains of fruits and vegetables, and we are really excited, but the best thing is that we are so close." The interviewer said, "What do you mean by close?" He said, "Well, we are only fourteen or fifteen years away."

In another vivid scene, a scientist explained that he had worked for seven years on a problem. The interviewer said, "What happened?" He said, "It didn't work." The interviewer said, "Well, what are you going to do now?" The scientist was walking down the hallway and turning off the light. As he left, he said, "I don't know." But the viewer had a very distinct feeling that that scientist would be back on Monday morning with a fresh approach to the problem and would keep on working.

Creativity is a process in which there are at least five phases:

1. *Preparation:* laying the groundwork and learning the background of the situation.
2. *Concentration:* becoming totally absorbed in the specific problem.
3. *Incubation:* taking time out, a rest period, and seeking distractions.
4. *Illumination:* the "Aha!" when we recognize the answer or discover an idea; the light bulb goes on.
5. *Verification:* confronting and solving the practical problems; other people hear, are persuaded, and enlisted; the work finally gets done through perseverance.

Any of these five phases can be interrupted by frustration, thwarted by detours, sent off course by taking the wrong trail, or turned around by a false idea, improper information, distortion, snarls, or knots.

The only way these problems can be solved is by hanging in there. Don Owens, Jr., said, "Many people fail in life because they believe in the adage: 'If you don't succeed, try something else.' But success eludes those who follow such advice. Virtually everyone has had dreams at one time or another, especially in youth. The dreams that came true did so because the people stuck to their ambitions. They refused to be discouraged. They never let disappointment get the upper hand. Challenges only spurred them on to greater effort."

I love the word "tenacity." It implies the courage to endure, which I believe is one of the greatest virtues that can be developed in any man or woman.

The following familiar statement by Calvin Coolidge is worth repeating because it is said so well (and "Silent Cal" was never known for using many words to say anything): "Nothing in the world can take the place of persistence. Talent will not; nothing is more common than unsuccessful men with talent. Genius will not; unrewarded genius is almost a proverb. Education will not; the world is full of educated derelicts. Persistence and determination alone are omnipotent. The slogan 'Press on' has solved, and always will solve, the problems of the human race."

In his superb book *Gold in the Making*, Ron Lee Davis relates the importance of tenacity in Christian faith. He tells the story of a missionary who visited a leprosarium:

As he was talking with some of the people there who were afflicted with this terrible disease, he met one particular leper who had a vital, glowing love for Jesus Christ. The two of them began to visit together.

The leper said to my friend, "You know, I didn't always have this joy, this love of God in my heart. When I first came to this Leprosarium I was the most angry, most bitter man here. But there was one man from the village nearby who came out every day to visit me. Every single day he came out and brought me food, and at first I threw it back in his face. He'd come out and offer to play cards with me, but I shouted at him to leave me alone. He wanted to talk with me, but I would have nothing to say to him. Still he kept coming to visit me, day after day after day after day."

Finally I could do nothing else but ask him, "Why? Why do you keep coming to see me, to love me, when all I ever show you is bitterness and hatred?"

And he told me it's because of the love of Jesus Christ Himself.

Then my friend asked the leper, "Well, how long did this man from the village come out to see you before you gave your heart to Christ?"

The leper answered, "He came every day for thirteen years."

Conclusion

The greatest miracle is the discovery that all is miraculous.
And the nature of the miraculous is—utter simplicity.

Whew! That's a lot of information. I hope these principles make sense to you and that you'll be able to use them in your problem-solving situations. It's a lot to remember, but as somebody said, "You can't memorize problem solving. You just need to take these tools and apply them to the places they best fit."

Maybe you'll need to keep this book handy so that you can refer back to these principles now and again. These principles certainly aren't meant to be used as a substitute for God's direction in our lives. They're simply tools that you can use to dig some space around your problems and get a proper perspective on them.

I read something recently that I thought might be an appropriate conclusion to this section. It's entitled "We Learned It All in Kindergarten," by Robert Fulghum, and it's a reminder that life isn't quite as complicated as we sometimes tend to make it.

Most of what I really need to know about how to live, and what to do, and how to be I learned in kindergarten. Wisdom was not at the top of the graduate-school mountain, but there in the sandbox.

These are the things I learned: Share everything. Play fair. Don't hit people. Put things back where you found them. Clean up your own mess. Don't take things that aren't yours. Say you're sorry when you hurt somebody. Wash your hands before you eat. Live a balanced life. Learn some and think some, and draw and sing and dance and play and work every day some.

Take a nap in the afternoon. When you go out into the world, watch for traffic, hold hands and stick together. Be aware of wonder. Remember the little seed in the plastic cup. The roots go down and the plant goes up, and nobody really knows why, but we are all like that.

Goldfish and hamsters and white mice and even the little seed in the plastic cup—they all die. So do we.

And then remember the book about Dick and Jane and the first word you learned, the biggest word of all: look. Everything you need to know is in there somewhere. The golden rule and love and basic sanitation. Ecology and politics and sane living.

Think of what a better world it would be if we all had cookies and milk about three o'clock every afternoon and then lay down with our blankets for a nap. Or if we had a basic policy in our nation and other nations always to put things back where we found them and cleaned up our own messes. And it is still true, no matter how old you are, when you go out into world, it is best to hold hands and stick together.

Part 3

Go for It!

14

Process: A Seven-Step Problem-Solving Process for All Occasions

The basic problem most people have is that they are doing nothing to solve their basic problem.

Bob Richardson

The world now has so many problems that if Moses had come down from Mount Sinai today the two tablets he'd carry would be aspirin.

Robert Orben

A man with fifty problems is twice as alive as a man with twenty-five. If you haven't got problems, you should get down on your knees and ask "Lord, don't you trust me anymore."

John Bainbridge

Is there a process for solving problems? The truth is there are many; there are countless ways to solve problems. In fact, there are probably as many ways to solve problems as there are people. It has helped me greatly, however, to be able to apply an objective problem-solving process to the problems that confront me. As is said in Aesop's fables, "Better one safe way than a hundred on which you cannot reckon."

I've seen three-step processes (stimulus, pause, response), four-step processes (preparation, incubation, illumination, verification), and various others. Some years ago, however, I stumbled across what I believe is an ingeniously simple seven-step problem-solving process that I think is the most complete and comprehensive system for problem solving that I've ever encountered.[1]

This seven-step process is appropriate to any problem whether it be fixing a kitchen door or a relationship at work, whether it be solving a logistical hassle or working with some disruption in your family. It works on all kinds of problems—and it is so logical that if you were to write these seven steps down and practice them, even for a few days, they would become automatic to you.

If you already have a process for problem solving that works for you, ignore this—but if you're curious, read on. A problem-solving process is something of a "window" to see through; its seven silhouetted steps can illuminate your awareness of the problem and your ability to articulate your journey through it.

---

[1] Numerous aspects of this seven-step process were taken from Curt Hanks et al., *Design Yourself!* (Los Altos, Calif.: William Kaufman, 1977). For those seeking further information, I highly recommend this book as well as Don Koberg and Jim Bagnall's *Universal Traveler: A Soft-Systems Guide to Creativity, Problem-Solving, and the Process of Reaching Goals,* rev. ed. (Los Altos, Calif.: William Kaufman, 1981).

The seven steps are listed below:

1. *Recognize and accept a problem.* You must first realize that a problem exists and be willing to engage yourself fully in an attempt to correct it. This, believe it or not, is one of most important steps in problem solving. It is the beginning point to all problem solving.

2. *Analyze the problem.* Take it apart, simplify it, get to know the ins and outs of the problem. See each of its pieces with as much clarity as possible.

3. *Define the problem.* What really is the problem? Eliminate anything that is unnecessary. What do you believe are the main issues of the problem? Clarify the major goals to solve the problem. It helps if you can write out the problem or state it clearly to another person.

4. *Brainstorm.* Generate as many ideas or potential answers as you can. If possible, brainstorm with another person. Write down every idea you think of. Quantity is more important than quality at this point.

5. *Select.* Choose what appears to be the best possible way of solving the problem at this time. Try to select between the best alternatives, taking the most logical solution at this time.

6. *Implement.* Try it out. Put into action your selected best choice.

7. *Evaluate.* Determine the effect or results of the solution in correcting the problem. Did it work? If not, what could you do to improve the solution at this time?

This means problem-solving is a continuing process or journey. If you finish the seven steps and are still unsatisfied, then you automatically go back to the beginning, to the first step, with a new sense of awareness. Remember that each of these steps or phases are *interrelated*, forming a continuous journey—the more we practice them the more natural they become. If we wish to improve our problem-solving abilities, we must work toward improving and developing each step or phase in the problem-solving process. Remember that the process of problem solving never really ends. The destinations or goals you achieve are merely rest stops along the bigger journey of life—so don't forget to enjoy the process.

Note that these seven steps are probably best designed in a circular format.

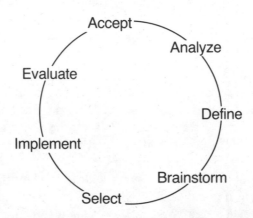

Step 1: *Acceptance.* We must accept responsibility for a problem before we can solve it. We cannot solve a problem by saying, "It's not my problem." We cannot solve a problem by hoping that someone else will solve it for us. We can only solve a problem when we say "this is my problem, and it's up to me to solve it." This step may seem obvious, but if any step in the problem-solving process is most critical, it would be this one. If we fail to accept a problem as ours, then all the other steps become meaningless. Our homes, work places, and newspapers are filled with tragic accounts of problems which are not accepted: take, for example, the alcoholic who doesn't believe he has a drinking problem, until he causes an accident in which someone is hurt or killed.

How many relationships and marriages break up because they have "communication" problems? Yet they never actually stopped and accepted it as a problem, meaning that they never actually tried to do something about the situation.

A problem is not a problem until you accept it as one. You must first *realize* that a problem exists and then *be willing to do something about it.* For example, in a seminary class recently I asked, "How many of you believe that world hunger is a problem?" Every hand went up. Then I asked, "How many of you are actually doing something about it?" Only a few hands went up. According to our problem-solving process, those who didn't raise their hands have not yet accepted hunger as a problem. To accept a problem means to change your energy state; it means that you are willing to do something, that you are ready to actively involve yourself in the problem-solving process. The first step in the problem-solving process is full acceptance or recognition that there *is* a problem.

Let's say that the muffler on your car has a hole in it causing it to make more noise than usual. If it doesn't bother you enough to do something about it, you don't have a problem. However, if a policeman stops you a week later to give you a ticket for faulty equipment on your automobile, you may then accept it as a problem. Then you begin the problem-solving process. To accept a problem means to make some change, to actually have that problem become a part of your life and to engage in the problem-solving process.

It has been said that loving is like boxing—in order to make contact, you have to get close enough to get hurt. The same is true for problem solving. In order to get close enough to affect the problem, you must be close enough for the problem to affect you. Thus, you must change your energy state from simply enduring the problem to attempting to solve it.

Again, this may all sound strange, but I might remind you that there are some very intelligent, gifted people who would rather live with problems, than accept the challenge of changing them or solving them. Acceptance is the first stage.

One final example: My wife, Pam, asked me, "When are you going to fix the back door?"

I said, "What door? It still opens. In fact, if you just put your toe under the outside corner and lift it a little as you close it—and then push the latch with your left thumb while you turn the knob with your right . . . it's 'no problem'!"

The door was not a problem to me. To Pam it was. The door didn't get fixed because I never accepted it as a problem. However, as you might have guessed, my wife eventually convinced me that the door really was a problem, and it finally got fixed.

Step 2: *Analyze the problem.*

The process of analysis is to pull the problem apart into its different elements, a great many of which you already know about. When you get it pulled completely apart, you can then work on the things you don't know about.

Charles Kettering

Charles Kettering was brilliant at analyzing problems. It was the key to most of his discoveries. He believed that if he carefully analyzed his problem he would discover that 90 percent of it had already been solved. He then had only to apply himself to the remaining 10 percent. Analyzing the problem is the second step or phase of problem solving. To analyze means to take the problem apart and carefully observe each of the pieces, to separate the larger problem into smaller bite-size ones, thus making the first problem less threatening.

The goal of analysis is to gain information, not to find an immediate solution. We need to get on intimate terms with the problem. We need to know if the problem is singular or if it is part of a much larger network. We also need to know if the problem is a chronic one or if this is the first time it has occurred.

To analyze is to investigate, to untangle, to untie the knot, to separate out the emotional aspects of the problem, to see how much "baggage" is perhaps attached to this problem. Investigate it from as many sides as possible. The key is your ability to design good questions.

Formulating good, solid questions will give you the information you need. Questions allow us to look at the problem from as many viewpoints as possible, but keep in mind that not all questions are equally appropriate. For example, the question "Why did this have to happen to me now?" is not a good question because it doesn't give you any information about the nature of the problem.

In the early 1960s, an interviewer was trying to get Ernest Hemingway to identify the essential characteristics of a "great" writer. As the interviewer offered various possibilities, Hemingway disparaged each. Finally, frustrated, the interviewer asked, "Isn't there at least one essential ingredient that you can identify?" Hemingway said, "In order to be a great writer a person must have a built-in, shock-proof, indestructible 'crap' detector."

I recommend such a detector for problem solving. It is a vital tool for separating the unnecessary, the clutter, and the baggage that distracts us from and confuses the real issue. I wish that I had discovered one sooner.

Is the problem still obscure to you? Is it blurred? What parts of the problem are relevant? What parts are irrelevant? Make the distinction between symptoms and the problem. A good question might be, "How does God see this problem?" Perhaps that would change your perspective in some way.

Mark Twain said, "Get your facts first, then you can distort them as you please." Take care not to twist the information you gain in the analytical phase either through predisposition or prejudice. The more accurate the information is at this stage, the better are our chances of finding the real problem and hence a solution that works. Simplify the problem as much as possible, break it down into its essential pieces and, if possible, establish priorities as you move toward a clear definition of what is truly at the core of the problem.

Step 3: *Definition.*

A problem well stated is a problem half solved.

Charles Kettering

All problems have central themes or major considerations. We call this the essence of the problem. A doctor questions you about certain symptoms in order to help him determine the cause of your illness. But you want him to cure the illness, not just your symptoms. He must solve the problem by attacking the real disease and not just the results it has caused.

Defining the problem, then, is almost as important as accepting the problem. What really is the problem? What is the essence of the problem? What do you believe the main issues of the problem to be? If you know what the problem is, you will find a solution easier. Albert Einstein said, "The formulation of a problem is far more essential than its solution."

All too often people try to solve a problem before they actually know what the problem is. Sometimes we want to remedy the result of the problem, its symptoms, instead of looking for and discovering the core of the problem. We waste so much time, expend so much energy and effort, only to achieve a partial or ineffective solution.

I told you earlier about an expert on problem solving who gave the following three suggestions for becoming a good problem solver. He said:

- Number 1, define your problem carefully.
- Number 2, redefine your problem carefully.
- Number 3, re-redefine your problem carefully.

In defining this step, we try to separate the essential from the nonessential. We try to establish a precise definition of what the problem really is. Again, it is critical to separate symptoms from problems.

I believe that it is very helpful to attempt to write the problem down. Putting it on paper somehow clarifies it. Another way to clarify your definition is to try to explain the problem to another person. By the way, if more than one person is involved in this problem, it is absolutely critical that each person involved in the problem be committed to the same definition. The best way to learn how to define problems effectively is to define them over and over and over again. The more you practice, the better you become.

Defining the problem is much like shooting at a bulls-eye target. You often know what the approximate problem is that you are to solve, just as you know where the target is, but hitting the exact bulls-eye is another thing. Sometimes it takes many tries before you are able to zero in on the true problem. Each time you shoot at defining the problem you get closer.[2]

Step 4: *The art of brainstorming.*

We don't know a millionth of one percent about anything.

Thomas Edison

---

[2] Hanks et al., *Design Yourself!* 95.

> Almost all really new ideas have a certain aspect of foolishness when they are first produced.
>
> *Alfred North Whitehead*

Brainstorming is the practice of obtaining ideas. Ideas don't just happen; you have to make them happen. As in any art, some skills and techniques will help make brainstorming more productive and successful.

A great scientist once said, "A way to have a good idea is to have lots of ideas."

The rules of brainstorming are simple: there are none. Creative ideas aren't limited to creative people. Brainstorming occurs anytime you turn your mind loose to think up all the wild possibilities to a problem, or better yet, when two or more get together to generate as many ideas as possible. "Originality," said Woodrow Wilson, "is simply a fresh pair of eyes." Now that you have carefully defined your problem, brainstorming should be an explosion of thought where you create as many wild ideas as possible.

Here are a few hints:

Think first—judge later. Sound simple? It is. By letting your mind run wild, you can eliminate all "blocks." Don't judge what you think. If you're in a group, don't say to yourself, "I won't say that because they'll think I'm stupid." Just let it out. Don't hold back any ideas. If you're brainstorming by yourself, write down on a piece of paper *everything* that comes to mind concerning the subject. Don't judge—we want *quantity*.

The wilder the ideas, the better. Let your mind get out of its everyday way of thinking, let it be creative. Off-beat and impractical ideas often trigger other ideas that can be very useful. "Hitchhike" off each other's thinking. Let others' thinking stimulate new ideas. Again, don't evaluate, don't judge, don't hold back any ideas because you think they're dumb. The wilder the better.

Quantity is wanted. The greater number of ideas you have the better chance you have of finding a winner. After a brainstorming session it's easy to eliminate useless or ridiculous ideas, but it is extremely difficult to puff up a short list of ideas. Without quantity you most likely will not find quality either. Cross-fertilize; think of ideas from as many different fields as possible.

Combine, improve, and expand ideas. I believe that the greatest thing that God has given us, outside of His Son, is each other. How often we get stuck with a problem and fail to go to a friend, or a team of friends, to brainstorm a possible solution or to try to clarify problems. If you want to improve your problem solving techniques, your parenting, your work, or any other area of your life, I could not encourage you more to get together with someone else and brainstorm the possibilities.

Suggest ways to expand the ideas of others. Carry any idea a little further, and make it a little better. Look for ways to combine two or more ideas to make an even better idea. Winston Churchill once said, "No idea is so outlandish that it should not be considered with a searching, but at the same time, steady eye."

I think that one of the most untapped resources in the kingdom of God is brainstorming. As it has been said, "seek and ye shall find." Most of the best ideas in the world haven't happened yet.

When you have an idea, write it down. Keep a notebook handy. You'll never know when you are going to get another idea. When Newton was asked how he came to understand gravity he said, "By thinking about it all the time." He had been pondering the problem for quite some time, and then one day while sitting under an apple tree, he saw an apple fall, and the concept of gravity came to him.

Many people laugh and say that when an apple falls it's obvious that gravity exists. But that's only because we live in an age familiar with Newton's theories. What Newton saw was the existence of strong attracting forces that caused the apple to fall, and from that he derived mathematical formulas and a theory of gravity thoroughly understood by relatively few people.

CLUSTERING

Idea getting, especially when you are by yourself, can be enhanced by a technique called "clustering."

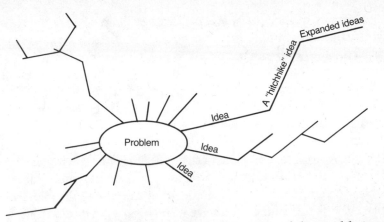

Put what you think is the clearest definition of the problem in the center of the page and then circle it. Then branch ideas like tree limbs off of the central core. Turn the pattern into a porcupine of ideas, letting each idea stimulate a new one. In this way, you "hitchhike" off your own ideas. Clustering is just another way of organizing your thoughts and of brainstorming by yourself. Try it, you'll like it!

Brainstorming is such an important tool for generating ideas that I thought it would be helpful for you to explore a few actual brainstorming situations:

- list ten ways you can improve your personal Bible study
- list twenty-five ways you can communicate "I Love You" to another person
- jot down fifteen ways to improve your child's education. If you don't have a child, choose a niece, nephew, grandchild, or friend
- think up nineteen ways to improve your job or work environment
- generate twenty-one ideas to increase your knowledge of a subject which interests you
- list twenty-six ways you can meet new people
- brainstorm seventeen ways you can improve a current relationship.[3]

---

[3] Norman Wakefield, *Solving Problems Before They Become Conflicts* (Grand Rapids, Mich.: Zondervan Publishing House, 1987).

Norman Wakefield suggests another helpful way to stretch your thinking: Simply gather several miscellaneous objects (such as a hat, a broom, or a plate). Have one person hold up the object and everyone think of as many new uses as they can for familiar objects. How many ways can it be modified, or adapted, or improved? Are there any ways to put two of the objects together to create a new object? Above all else, have fun.

Step 5: *Select.* The next obvious (that's what I like about this process) step is to select the best possible way of solving the problem from the list of ideas and alternatives you've created from your brainstorming sessions. Remember that the more information you have, the better chance you have of making a good selection.

You cannot drink from a dry well. So be inquisitive. Ask questions. Compare and contrast the various options you have. Set up some criterion for determining the best choice. How to select the best alternative is as important as how much information you have gathered. Establish a priority list based on the quality and usefulness of each idea. Once you've narrowed down your possibilities, make a choice.

To be truly effective, your selected choice should be consistent with your core values (i.e., is your selected solution consistent with your long term goals and priorities?) Make sure that your choice is not based simply on what is most convenient. Be as objective as possible in selecting the best option, and then . . .

Step 6: *Implement.*

The vaults of heaven are filled with good opportunities, the vaults of hell with good intentions.

Implementation is, of course, the next logical step in the sequence. Again, this whole seven-step process is so logical and comprehensive that with a little bit of use, you will remember it easily. Now is the time to give action, or physical form, to your "selected best choice." Now's the time to translate theory into reality. We have planned our work, now we must work our plan. You must leave the safety of the blackboard and enter in the wilderness of practical experience. You can read a map, select numerous alternative routes forever, but at some point in time, you must put on your boots and set out.

How you implement your plan is totally up to you—but this is the time to act. Suppose you had to tell a girlfriend or boyfriend that you were no longer going to go out with her or him. You have a number of ways to implement it. You could tell him or her directly, notify them through a brother or sister, have a mutual friend tell them, or slip it to them by note. But the key is action. There is no substitute for actually doing it. There is no way of fully knowing before implementation and actually experiencing your choice. It has been said, "to know and not to act is to not know."

If you worry about what might be, or wonder about what might have been, you will continually ignore what is. The "catch" is we only develop the skills and expertise in problem solving by solving problems. Kathy Seligman, a journalist, once said, "You can't hit a home run unless you step up to the plate. You can't catch fish unless you put your line into the water. You can't reach your goals unless you actually do something." Similarly, Yoda, the little green master of wisdom, said in *The Empire Strikes Back*, "Try? There is no try. There is only do or not do." Now is the time to do.

Once you've taken action, you are ready for the final step in the problem-solving process—which is to . . .

Step 7: *Evaluate.*

> Evaluations are not conclusion; they are commencements. They end one journey and carry us on to the more knowledgeable beginning of another journey. Just as commencement means both to complete and to begin, so evaluation is the link between our problem solving journeys.

When problems arise to complicate an already busy day, many times I tend to skip this stage of the process and begin on work on one of the many other problems I've accepted. When I give into this temptation, I miss much of what the problem solving process has to teach me. Therefore, I would encourage you not to compromise on your education.

Ask yourself, "Did it work?" Now is the time for accounting, for comparing the beginning with the end, for detecting flaws and discoveries, and possibly for planting the seeds of future challenges. You must at this point determine the effects and ramifications of your problem-solving process. Is your solution workable? Is it the best you can possibly do at this time? If it is, then you've completed the process, and you're ready for something new. If not, you perhaps need to return to step 1 and begin the process all over again. Here's a small list of questions that you might want to consider in your evaluation process.

1. What about the solution proved effective?
2. What would have made the solution more effective?
3. Were there any unexpected benefits or liabilities?
4. Which skills need to be acquired or improved?
5. Who else could benefit from this solution?
6. Can this solution be used to prevent a recurrence of the problem?
7. What was learned from the process of solving this problem?

The whole seven-step design is a learning process. The more we practice it, the more natural it becomes. If we wish to improve our problem-solving abilities, we must work toward improving and developing each step or phase of the creative problem-solving process. But remember, the problem-solving process never really ends. Destinations or goals achieved are merely rest stops along the bigger journey of life—so don't forget to enjoy the process.

Use this problem-solving process in your everyday life. You might be surprised to discover a new sense of clarity and direction unfolding in your life. Remember, the test of character isn't always how we handle the big problems but how we deal with the ordinary ones as well.

This seven-step procedure is only a process, an approach, a form. The substance and essential focus of our problem solving still needs to be on what God is saying to us. In order to hear what He is saying we must take the time to listen for His voice.

> I got up early one morning
> And rushed right into the day;
> I had so much to accomplish
> That I didn't have time to pray.

Problems came tumbling about me
And heavier came each task
"Why doesn't God help?" I wondered;
He answered, "You didn't ask."

I wanted to see joy and beauty
But the day toiled on gray and bleak;
I wondered why God didn't show me
He said, "But you didn't seek."

I tried to come into God's presence;
I used all my keys at the lock
God gently and lovingly chided
"My child, you didn't knock."

I woke early this morning
And paused before entering the day;
I had so much to accomplish,
That I had to take time to pray.

15

Experience: The Essential Component

A football coach will admonish his players that how well they practice is how well they'll perform in the game. To anticipate the other team's moves, to make their own moves habitual, players have to do three things: practice . . . practice . . . practice.

Until now, we've been talking about how to apply principles to problem solving. I know I've given you a ton of information, and I hope that these principles make sense to you and that you'll use them in your problem-solving situations.

Frederick Bueckner said, "Principles are what people have instead of God." These principles aren't those kind of principles and certainly aren't meant to be used as a substitute for God's ability to work in our lives. They are simply tools that you can use to dig some space around your problems and get a proper perspective on them.

Just remember, all the principles in the world won't solve your problems for you. You have to solve them yourselves, using those principles. There is simply no substitute for good old hard work and lots of on-the-job training, otherwise known as experience.

> Has any man ever obtained inner harmony by simply reading about the experiences of others? Not since the world began has it ever happened. Each man must go through the fire himself.
>
> *Norman Douglas*

> Never measure the height of a mountain until you have reached the top. Then you will see how low it was.
>
> *Dag Hammarskjold*

> Truth divorced from experience will always dwell in the realms of doubt.
>
> *Henry Krause*

The concordance to my New International Version of the Bible contains no listing for "experience." Where experience should be there is a gap that jumps from "expensive" to "expert." But this is actually consistent with what experience is. No one can tell you; you have to find it on your own.

If problem solving is to become one of your habits, something you do instinctively, then there is nothing more crucial than practice. All the preceding information on seven-step process, attitudes, and principles are nothing more than good ideas unless we test their worth in our day-to-day living.

As a youth, I applied for a part-time job in a small department store in the center of the town where I lived. The elderly man who owned the store squinted at me through his bifocals and asked, "You got any experience, son?"

I said, "Well, I . . ."

"I mean in a department store like this one," he interrupted.

"Well, maybe not exactly like this one, but . . . ," I said.

"'Cuz we don't hire anyone who don't have no experience," he said.

"Well, I was hoping to get a little experience here," I replied.

The store owner shook his head, "I'm sorry, son, but we don't hire anyone who don't have no experience."

Experience is expensive. It takes time, effort, and sometimes failure to acquire this precious commodity. I am certain that if any of us could find ways around having to get experience, we would leap at the opportunity. There is, however, only one road to expertise in any field, and that is the road over the peaks and valleys of trial and error.

New techniques, however, can be risky, especially if our problem is somewhat threatening. Therefore, it is best to gain your experience in arenas where the stakes are not quite as high, where you feel less threatened.

Thomas Edison, who believed in creative problem solving, frequently used his times of relaxation to play with puzzles. So to gain that experience let's solve some puzzles.

Puzzles require us to work our minds backwards and forwards. The benefit is that in working our minds, we stretch our capabilities and tone up our creative fiber. Many of the following exercises will help you break up the rigid structures built into your thought processes. Thus they can enhance your ability to solve those problems that come your way in less-than-conventional terms.

The exercises in this chapter will give you an opportunity to gain experience in solving different types of problems. Some of these will seem quite easy for you while others will seem more difficult. The experience you gain is definitely transferable to your problems in the real world.

But please don't use these exercises as a measure of your intelligence or abilities. That is not their purpose. These exercises are simply an arena in which you can learn to solve problems better. Remember, you solve problems better when you're having fun. Enjoy!

If at first you don't succeed, you're about average!

Dr. Robert Anthony

1. A man was born in the year 50 B.C. How old was he on his birthday in 50 A.D.?

2. One side of an isosceles triangle is 12 inches; another is 5 inches. What is the length of the third side?

3. When is it legal in Kentucky for a man to marry his daughter? What are all the possible combinations in this answer? Which ones are reasonable? What assumptions are you making?

4. Can you work out in your head, without the help of a pencil, the answer to this age-old riddle?

   > As I was going to St. Ives,
   > I met a man with seven wives,
   > Each wife had seven cats,
   > Each cat had seven kittens.
   > How many were going to St. Ives?

5. A circular cake is cut into eight equal parts using only three cuts with a knife. How can this happen? How many different ways can this happen?

Go beyond the first right solution. Look for other right answers. One of the prime common denominators among creative thinkers is that they see multiple solutions to any one given problem. This trait, however, is a learned skill, so keep practicing.

6. How many triangles are in the figure below?

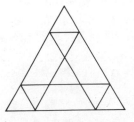

Remember Number ten! Keep looking.

7. Name the color that is concealed in each sentence. In this series of problems it will be important for you to see these sentences a little differently. This will test your ability to see beyond the obvious. Example: The newspaper *ed*itors decided to go on strike. *Answer*: Red. The ca*b lack*ed proper brakes to stop at the intersection. *Answer*: Black.

   Now try these:

   a. Having older siblings was a distinct advantage to Roger.
   b. The cop persuaded him not to create a disturbance.
   c. Sheri wanted to yell, "Owe them nothing except love and kindness."
   d. This tool, I've been led to believe, is the best in the world.
   e. No other city in the world can match Rome's significance.
   f. The customs here are both different and wonderful.
   g. When it came to singing, Ray couldn't carry a tune in a bucket with a lid on it.
   h. The fossil Vern found was not only old, but valuable.
   i. After school, I laced up footballs to earn extra money.
   j. Sue decided it would be better to appear last.

These next few exercises will challenge your ability to analyze problems. If you get stuck, take a few minutes and let your mind relax. You may be surprised by how well you do when you allow your mind to relax.

8. There are four volumes of Shakespeare's collected works on the shelf. The pages of each volume are exactly 2″ thick. The covers are each ⅙″ thick. The bookworm started eating on page 1 of volume 1 and ate through to the last page of volume 4. What is the distance the bookworm covered?

9. How many answers can you think of to this question: What is half of 13? Of course, the obvious one is 6.5. See if you can find other acceptable answers. This exercise is not easy, but don't be discouraged. Chances are you can stump your friends with it.

   In creative problem solving, it is frequently more important to look at a problem from different vantage points rather than run with the first solution that pops into your head.

   Eugene Raudsepp

10. *Time and Tide.* A ship is at anchor. Over its side hangs a rope ladder with its rungs a foot apart. The tide rises at a rate of 8 inches per hour. At the end of six hours, how much of the rope ladder will remain above the water, assuming that eight feet were above water when the tide began to rise? Be sure you are keeping a broad enough perspective and that you are using all the information at your disposal.

11. A snail is at the bottom of a thirty-foot well. It can crawl upward three feet a day, but at night it slips back two feet. How long does it take the snail to crawl out of the well? Are you following the problem all the way through?

12. A hunter arose early, ate breakfast, and headed south. Half a mile from the camp he fell and skinned his nose. He picked himself up, frustrated, and continued south. Half a mile further along, he spotted a bear. Drawing a bead, he pulled the trigger, but the safety was on. Before he could get the safety off the bear attacked and ate him. Just kidding! The bear saw him and headed east at top speed. Half a mile later the hunter caught up, fired, but only wounded the beast, which limped off toward the east. The hunter followed and half a mile later caught and killed the bear. Pleased, the hunter walked the mile north back to his camp to find it had been ransacked by a second bear. What color is the bear that tore up his camp?

13. A child playing on the beach had 6 1/6 sand piles in one place and 3 1/3 in another. If he put them all together, how many would he have?

14. Which book in the Bible records the murder of Cain by Abel?

15. When you take two apples from three apples, what do you have?

16. John is Dr. Johnson's son, but Dr. Johnson is not John's father. How do you explain this?

17. A country squire living on his farm is served two fresh eggs every morning. He does not own any hens; he does not buy, beg, or steal the eggs; he does not trade for them or find them, and he is not presented with them. Where do the eggs come from?

18. How many times can you subtract 2 from the numeral 21?

19. Read the following sentence once, slowly, counting the number of Fs.

> Final files are the result
> of years of scientific
> study with the experience
> of years.

How many did you find?

20. A single English word can be formed from these letters. What is it? Use all the letters:

pnlleeeesssss

21. Can you move three circles and turn the triangle upside down?

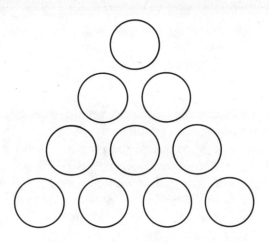

22. A glass is depicted by four matches, and an ice cube is represented by a penny. Can you put the ice cube in the glass by moving only two matches?

Be aware of how you go about solving your problems. Even wrong solutions can give you insights into good problem-solving strategies.

23. A hole in the ground is 3 feet long, 1½ feet wide, and 6 inches deep, how much earth does it contain?

24. Make the following equation valid by moving only one line.

$$VII + VII = VIII$$

People who see multiple solutions sometimes experience greater difficulty with these type of problems.

There is a story told of one of the pioneers of IQ testing who, after spending much time developing his particular test for intelligence, was confronted by colleagues who said his test was inaccurate. They said that very intelligent people could find more than one right answer to many of the questions used in the test. But the scientist was not willing to believe it. After much argument and discussion, the dissenting scientist was asked to take his own test. He did so and got a horribly low score.

His colleagues pointed out that he was scored according to valid but alternate answers to his questions. While it is important to see all the possibilities, we can sometimes save a lot of effort by testing the simplest solutions first.

AIRPLANES FROM WHACK

A group of engineers were brought together and asked to make a paper object that would fly a distance of twenty feet with the best possible accuracy. A sizable bonus was offered to whomever came up with the most successful design. After the engineers completed their designs, they took turns flying their creations across the room.

On each design's first flight, its landing spot was marked with colored tape, and these distances were measured. None were able to repeat flights with accuracy, and the engineers' frustration mounted.

Finally, one engineer approached the test area, wadded up her design into a ball, and threw it across the room. Then she very calmly marked its landing point with her colored tape, picked up the ball of paper, and proceeded to repeat the process with great accuracy.

When her fellow engineers cried foul, she reminded them of the criteria by which all their designs were being judged: it must fly twenty feet across the room with the greatest amount of accuracy possible. Her paper ball flew twenty feet landed within eight inches of the first landing every time.

I picked up many of these exercises while teaching at Menlo-Atherton High School in the San Francisco Bay area. While there, I had the privilege of teaching a class for the supposedly educationally handicapped. I say "supposedly" because many of these kids were very bright, but public education had simply failed to arouse their natural curiosity.

I found an experiment in the graduate program at Stanford University and introduced it to my students. The experiment was to find a way to drop an egg ten feet without breaking it. The parameters of the experiment were simple: once the egg was released from the roof, the egg could not in any way be touched by human hands until after it came to rest on the ground. These kids became so caught up in this experiment that for three days they showed up early for class and stayed after school just to work on it.

In the flurry of effort, only Eddie remained inactive. Eddie was the one who struggled the most with school. When I asked him if he needed any help, he would just smile and say, "No problem! I got it."

By the third day, such projects as spiral troughs and chutes made out of cardboard, styrofoam landing crafts attached to parachutes, and many other designs were nearing completion. I was amazed at their inventiveness. Still, I was concerned for Eddie. He hadn't made a move to construct anything. Whenever one of the other kids asked him what he was going to do, he would just laugh and say, "Hey, I got it man. I got it."

That afternoon, we began testing all the different designs that had been made. Eggs rolled down ramps and into cushioned boxes. Eggs floated down in landing crafts. Some crash-landed under parachutes that had failed to open. When all the designs had been tested, with a remarkable success rate, I turned to Eddie and said, "Well Sport, what have you got."

Eddie grinned, took an egg, climbed up the ladder to the roof, and walked over to the edge. Everyone watched and wondered what Eddie would do.

"You ready?" he said.

"Yeah! Come on Eddie. Do it!" the students yelled.

Eddie stuffed the egg into his mouth (thus, he had "released" it from his hand) and jumped off the roof. The egg arrived unharmed.

What are educationally handicapped kids but kids that education has failed to reach! These students were, by the way, highly successful at many of the exercises found in this chapter. In fact, they became so interested in these "think things," as I called them, that their attendance rose dramatically. I should add, however, that it wasn't always simply for the joy of problem solving. Many of these kids would take these exercises to the streets and make money by betting people that they couldn't solve them.

In education, we are often so committed to teaching answers that we forget to encourage people to a fuller understanding of process. Yet in our society, one of the most startling realities we face by the time students graduate is that most of what they've learned will one day be obsolete. The emphasis in our educational system needs to shift from what to think to how to think.

SAY IT CREATIVELY

Saying things in roundabout ways, with excessively large or unnecessary words is not the way to write. Many people are guilty of it, however, since they consciously or unconsciously wish to sound educated. A test for good writing is called the "Fog Index." This test favors writings with short sentences using short, simple, well-known words. It disapprobates polysyllabic sesquipedalian, tautological, redundant, periphrastic circumlocution because that is harder to read and understand.

Here is a collection of common proverbs rewritten until they have a horrible fog index. Challenging reading, they also make fun small-group exercises. (Divide up in small groups and see which group can make sense of the sesquipedalian proverbial paraphrastic circumlocution first.) At any rate, you will want to keep a collegiate dictionary close at hand; you never know when you may meet a sesquipedalian, and a dictionary will be your only defense.

SESQUIPEDALIAN PROVERBIAL PARAPHRASTIC
CIRCUMLOCUTION

1. Scintillate, scintillate, asteroid minific.
2. Members of an avian species of identical plumage congregate.
3. Surveillance should precede saltation.
4. Pulchritude possesses solely cutaneous profundity.
5. It is fruitless to become lachrymose over precipitately departed lacteal fluid.
6. Freedom from incrustations of grime is contiguous to rectitude.
7. The stylus is more potent than the claymore.
8. It is fruitless to attempt to indoctrinate a superannuated canine with innovative maneuvers.
9. Eschew the implement of correction and vitiate the scion.
10. The temperature of the aqueous content of an unremittingly ogled saucepan does not reach 212 degrees F.
11. All articles that coruscate with resplendence are not aurum.
12. Where there are visible vapors having their prevalence in ignited carbonaceous materials, there is conflagration.
13. Sorting on the part of mendicants must be interdicted.
14. A plethora of individuals with expertise in culinary techniques vitiate the potable concoction produced by steeping certain comestibles.
15. Eleemosynary deeds have their incipience intramurally.
16. Male cadavers are incapable of yielding any testimony.
17. Individuals who make their abode in vitreous edifices would be advised to refrain from catapulting petrous projectiles.
18. Neophytes serendipity.
19. Exclusive dedication to necessitous chores without interludes of hedonistic diversion renders John a hebetudinous fellow.
20. A revolving lithic conglomerate accumulates no congeries of a minuscule, verdant bryophytic plant.

21. The person presenting the ultimate cachinnation possesses thereby the optimal cachinnation.
22. Abstention from any aleatory undertakings precludes a potential escalation of a lucrative nature.
23. Missiles of ligneous or petrous consistency have the potential of fracturing my osseous structure, but appellations will eternally remain innocuous.
24. Persons of imbecilic mentality deviate in parameters which cherubic entities approach with trepidation.
25. Elementary sartorial techniques initially applied preclude repetitive similar actions to square of three.
26. A feline donning appendage-protecting accessories apprehends zero petite rodents.
27. Desist from enumerating your fowl prior to their emergence from the prenatal ovoid structure.
28. Disposition to inquiry deprived the feline of its vital state.
29. It is practicable to entice an *Equus caballus* to a reservoir of liquid hydrogen oxide but coercing him to imbibe is insuperable.
30. Upon the nonpresence of the domestic *Felis catus* the *Mus musculi* proceed to engage in sportive capers.
31. A buffoon and his accumulation of legal tender are expeditiously disunited.
32. Exigency is the matriarch of ingenious contrivance.

WORDELS

Here is an exercise to eliminate your habitual thinking patterns, pull you up out of your mental rut, and stretch your thinking powers.

This task requires you to take a different point of view, make the familiar strange and simplify what appears to be a complex problem. Try to figure out what common phrase or word is depicted in each puzzle.

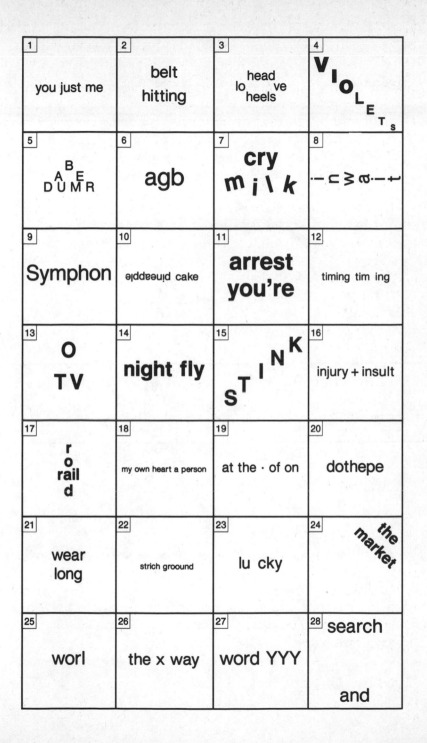

1	2	3	4
you just me	belt hitting	head lo ve heels	VIOLETs

5	6	7	8
B A E D U M R	agb	cry m i l k	i u w a i t

9	10	11	12
Symphon	pineapple cake	arrest you're	timing tim ing

13	14	15	16
O TV	night fly	STINK	injury + insult

17	18	19	20
r o rail d	my own heart a person	at the · of on	dothepe

21	22	23	24
wear long	strich grround	lu cky	the market

25	26	27	28
worl	the x way	word YYY	search and

29 go off coc	**30** no ways it ways	**31** oholene	**32** t o e a r t h
33 ooo circus	**34** 1 at 3:46	**35** late n e v e r	**36** get a word in
37 let gone gone be gone gone	**38** a chance n	**39** O MD BA PhD	**40** wheather
41 world world world world	**42** lo ose	**43** HE AD AC HE	**44** chicken
45 y fireworks	**46** L D Bridge	**47** danc t e s c etno	**48** EZ / iii
49 T O U C H	**50** MOTH cry cry cry	**51** BLACK / COAT	**52** TIME TIME
53 S A N D	**54** Hurry ↗	**55** MeQuit	**56** Le vel

57 KNEE / Light	**58** Man / Board	**59** He's / Himself	**60** R|E|A|D|I|N|G
61 AGES	**62** R ROAD A D	**63** DICE DICE	**64** ECNALG
65 cycle cycle cycle	**66** CHAIR	**67** T O W N	**68** iii iii o o
69 STAND / I	**70** THINGS R ↑ THINGS R THINGS R	**71** THOUGHT AN	**72** DON'T / XIOD
73 Take It / Yourself	**74** GRE / AT	**75** GOITITITIT	**76** BbBbbB
77 ESTIMATE Yourself / DON'T	**78** B A S L E E P G	**79** HEAR TED / GNIKAERB	**80** ACт
81 10 Don't	**82** BAN ANA	**83** F O L O	**84** BUSY BUSY

This final problem is a great exercise in logical deduction. It will test your ability to pull together various bits of information and come up with a correct solution.

WHO OWNS THE ZEBRA

There are five houses, each painted with a different color, and inhabited by men of different nationalities, with different pets, drinks, and cigarettes.

1. The Englishman lives in a red house.
2. The Spaniard owns a dog.
3. The Ukrainian drinks tea.
4. Coffee is drunk in the green house.
5. The green house is immediately to the right (your right) of the ivory house.
6. The Old Gold smoker owns snails.
7. Milk is drunk in the middle house.
8. The Norwegian lives in the first house on the left.
9. Kools are smoked in the yellow house.
10. The man who smokes Chesterfields lives in the house next to the man with the fox.
11. Kools are smoked in the house next to the house where the horse is kept.
12. The Lucky Strike smoker drinks orange juice.
13. The Japanese smokes Parliaments.
14. The Norwegian lives next to the blue house.

The Problem: Who owns the zebra and who drinks the water.

I could go on and on with puzzles and problems, but I think you get the idea. If we're going to solve the problems that come our way, we have to practice problem solving regularly. The best devices I have found for practice have been in books such as:

Jim Fixx, Games for the Super-Intelligent (Garden City, N.Y.: Doubleday and Company, 1972)

L. H. Longley-Cook, Fun for Puzzle People (New York: Fawcett Books, 1977); and More Puzzle Fun (New York: Fawcett Books, 1979)

Herman Hover, *How Many Three Cent Stamps in a Dozen?*
(Los Angeles, Calif.: Price Stern Sloan, 1976)
Eugene Raudsepp and George P. Hough, Jr., *Creative Growth Games* (San Diego, Calif.: Harvest Books, 1977)

but I would also point you toward your area bookstores which have numerous books of puzzles and brain teasers.

ANSWERS

1. 99, there is no year 0 A.D. or B.C. Remember to see all that is there! Take into consideration all the information that is given. It is important that you give yourself enough time to deal effectively with the problem.[1]

2. 12 inches. An isosceles triangle must have two sides that are equal. If you got 13, you where thinking of a right triangle (the hypotenuse squared being equal to the sum of the squares of the other two sides $[a^2 + b^2 = c^2]$). Are you defining the problem correctly? Are you giving your problem its proper definition? This exercise illustrates one of the most common errors made in our "get-it-done-yesterday" society: our tendency to push through to a solution of a problem that we haven't properly defined.

3. When the man is a justice of the peace, clergyman, pastor, or a rabbi. An important problem-solving technique is to be aware of how you define the different components of a problem. Wrong definitions will mean wrong solutions.

4. There is only one going to St. Ives. The other 344 are coming from St. Ives. This is a good exercise to get wrong. Many times the key to solving a problem results from separating information that is important from information that is unnecessary. When we fail to do this, we can be fooled by the environment in which the problem is presented.

---

[1]Numbers 1 through 6 are from L. H. Longley-Cook, *More Puzzle Fun* (New York: Fawcett Books, 1979).

5. Cut the cake in half, align the two halves one above the other and cut them both with a single cut, and then align the four quarters prior to the third and final cut. Or, first quarter the cake and then make a horizontal cut halfway up the height of the cake.

6. 14.

7. gold, copper, yellow, olive, chrome, tan, gray, silver, lilac, pearl.[2]

8. 5″. As the books are lined up on the shelf, page one of volume one is 2⅙″ from the end of the stack leaving only 5″ from page one of volume one to the last page in volume four. What were your assumptions? Did you challenge them before looking up the answer?

9. 1, 2, 3, 4, 6.5, 8, and 11. Divide the 1 and 3, if you add them together you get 4. If you write it as a Roman numeral and divide it (XI/II), you get 11 and 2. Split the same Roman numeral horizontally, and you get a mirror image Roman numeral 8 (XIII). [OK, so I was reaching to get 4!]

10. In that the boat rises with the tide, eight feet will remain above water.[3]

11. On the twenty-eighth day the snail reaches the top of the well and doesn't slide down.

12. The only way to follow the directions given and end up back at his camp would be if the camp were at the North Pole. Therefore, the bear must be a polar bear and as such would be white.

13. One. If you got tripped up by this one, you may be trying to

---

[2] Questions 7 through 9 are from Eugene Raudsepp and George P. Hough, Jr., *Creative Growth Games* (San Diego, Calif.: Harvest Books, 1977).

[3] Questions 10 through 12 are from Jim Fixx, *Games for the Super-Intelligent* (Garden City, N.Y.: Doubleday & Co., 1972); this particular exercise also appears in Herman Hover, *How Many Three Cent Stamps in a Dozen?* (Los Angeles, Calif.: Price Stern Sloan, 1976).

push through these a little too quickly. Remember good problem solving requires time.[4]

14. None—Cain murdered Abel. This one can be a bit of a groaner; you may feel more tricked than stumped. But this illustrates another one of the more common pitfalls in problem solving: our tendency to make assumptions when faced with a "common knowledge" issue.

15. Whatever you had before plus two apples.

16. Dr. Johnson is John's mother.

17. Ducks

18. Only once—from then on, you would be subtracting from 19 and then 17 and so on.

19. If you spotted four you're above average. And if you counted five, you can turn up your nose at almost everybody. Six is perfect.

20. Sleeplessness.

21.[5]

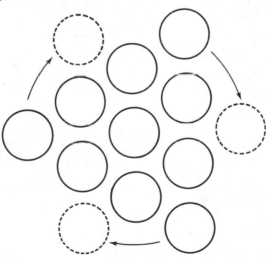

---

[4]Questions 13 through 20 are from Hover, *How Many Three Cent Stamps in a Dozen?*

[5]Questions 21 through 24 are from Longley-Cook, *Fun for Puzzle People* (New York: Fawcett Books, 1977).

22.

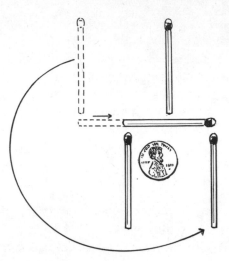

23. No earth at all, only air.
24. Make the equal sign into an inequality. If you are saying to yourself, "Oh come on! There must be a better answer," you're right.

SESQUIPEDALIAN PROVERBIAL PARAPHRASPIC CIRCUMLOCUTION

1. Twinkle, twinkle little star.
2. Birds of a feather flock together.
3. Look before you leap.
4. Beauty is only skin deep.
5. It does no good to cry over spilt milk.
6. Cleanliness is next to Godliness.
7. The pen is mightier than the sword.
8. You can't teach an old dog new tricks.
9. Spare the rod and spoil the child.
10. A watched pot never boils.
11. All that glitters is not gold.
12. Where there's smoke, there's fire.
13. Beggars can't be choosers.
14. Too many cooks spoil the broth.
15. Charity begins at home.
16. Dead men tell no tales.

17. People who live in glass houses shouldn't throw stones.
18. Beginner's luck.
19. All work and no play make Jack a dull boy.
20. A rolling stone gathers no moss.
21. He who laughs last laughs best.
22. Nothing ventured, nothing gained.
23. Sticks and stones may break my bones, but words can never hurt me.
24. Fools step in where angels fear to tread.
25. A stitch in time saves nine.
26. A cat in mittens catches no mice.
27. Don't count your chickens before they hatch.
28. Curiosity killed the cat.
29. You can lead a horse to water, but you can't make him drink.
30. When the cat is away, the mice will play.
31. A fool and his money are soon parted.
32. Necessity is the mother of invention.

WORDELS

1. Just between you and me
2. Hitting below the belt
3. Head over heels in love
4. Shrinking violet
5. Bermuda triangle
6. Mixed bag
7. Cry over spilled milk
8. Lying in wait
9. Unfinished symphony
10. Pineapple upside-down cake
11. You're under arrest
12. Split-second timing
13. Nothing on TV
14. Fly by night
15. Stuck up
16. Adding insult to injury
17. Railroad crossing
18. A person after my own heart
19. At the point of no return

20. The inside dope
21. Long underwear
22. Ostrich with its head in the ground
23. Lucky break
24. Cornering the market
25. World without end
26. Something in the way
27. Word wise
28. Search high and low
29. Go off half cocked
30. No two ways about it
31. A hole in one
32. Down to earth
33. Three-ring circus
34. One at a time
35. Better late than never
36. Get a word in edgewise
37. Let bygones be bygones
38. An outside chance
39. Three degrees below zero
40. A bad spell of weather
41. Worlds apart
42. Break loose
43. Splitting headache
44. Chicken Little
45. Fourth of July fireworks
46. London Bridge
47. Square dance contest
48. Easy on the eyes
49. Touchdown
50. Moth balls
51. Black overcoat
52. Time after time
53. Sandslide
54. Hurry up
55. Quit following me
56. Split level

57. Neon light
58. Man overboard
59. He's beside himself
60. Reading between the lines
61. Dark Ages
62. Crossroads
63. Paradise
64. Backward glance
65. Tricycle
66. Highchair
67. Uptown downtown
68. Circles under the eyes
69. I understand
70. Things are looking up
71. An afterthought
72. Don't overextend
73. Take it upon yourself
74. The great divide
75. Go for it
76. Bee line
77. Don't underestimate yourself
78. Down sleeping bag
79. Broken hearted over breaking up
80. Disappearing act
81. Don't pretend
82. Banana split
83. Fool around
84. Too busy

WHO OWNS THE ZEBRA

First house: yellow, Norwegian, Kools, water, fox. Second House: blue, Ukrainian, Chesterfields, tea, horse. Third house: red, Englishman, Old Golds, milk, snails. Fourth house: ivory, Spaniard, Lucky Strikes, orange juice, dog. Fifth house: green, Japanese, Parliaments, coffee, Zebra. Thus, the Japanese owns the zebra, and the Norwegian drinks the water.

Part 4

Reality—What
a Concept!

16

Unsolvable Problems

Some wishes cannot succeed; some victories cannot be won;
some loneliness is incorrigible. The only relief and freedom
is in knowing what is real.

Wendell Berry

In this life we will encounter hurts and trials that we will not
be able to change; we are just going to have to allow them to
change us.

Ron Lee Davis

I got the message this afternoon. I didn't expect it. I didn't want
it. It was so sudden, so final, so unsolvable! I couldn't stop it. Don
Anderson has been a dear friend for such a long time. He and his
wife, Jacque, were genuine examples of what the Christian life is
supposed to be about. Their kindness and compassion were un-
bounded.

I still remember vividly the night 120 wild and wonderful high
school kids jammed every corner of the Andersons' living room.
Their home had an open door for anyone who needed hope or

love. Their kitchen was a center of conversation, a place for anyone who was hurting or struggling to receive comfort. Their home was filled not only with their own joy but also with that of Christ.

When I first met Don and Jacque, I was a struggling Young Life leader living on $200 a month. Don and Jacque gave me a room above their garage. They welcomed me into their family. They shared their meals with me. Their love was displayed toward me in a very practical manner: bacon and eggs on Tuesday morning, a reading from Proverbs (Don's favorite book), cookies and milk at midnight, and constant open arms for whatever stray and lonely kid I'd happen to run into.

When Summit Expedition had its first course in 1970, Don and Jacque invited the entire group of kids who were on that course home for dinner. Don made each person feel like he or she was one of his own children. Jacque served so much food I finally decided it was a seven-course meal especially designed for hungry kids who had just spent twenty-three days in the wilderness eating dried food.

Both Don and Jacque worked full time outside the home, but they were also committed to full-time ministry, too. Their home seemed to me to be a genuine extension of the church.

I was blessed beyond measure to be a part of their lives and home. I wouldn't have made it through those special years without their generosity (and that of other families like Ed and Lillian Dixson's).

. . . I got the message this afternoon. I didn't expect it. I didn't want it. It was so sudden, so final, so unsolvable! I couldn't stop it. Don had just died.

The problem with some problems is that they can't be solved. It is a problem for me and for Jacque and for others who loved him so much that Don is now gone home to be with his Maker. All the problem-solving skills and all the principles and processes won't bring him back to be with us. We'll never firsthand enjoy his presence again, at least not in this life. And that is sad. Even though we know he is with God, we are still sad that he is not here with us.

Some problems such as this one will remain unresolved. Some hopes will never be fulfilled. Some dreams will never be accomplished. Some problems are just not meant to be solved in this life.

Jesus promised us joy and eternal life, and He Promised us that He would always be with us. But remember this: joy is not the same as happiness. Jesus did not promise that a Christian's life would be free of troubles and problems. He did not promise us happiness, health, or success. Nor did He promise that our relationships would last forever. Pain like that I experienced over Don's death is inseparable from human life.

A friend of mine was born with a serious handicap. As if that weren't enough, she also lives with a life-long scar from the memory of being sexually abused as a child. And because her parents died when she was eighteen, she is alone in the world with her incessant pain and dreadful memories. When I talk to her, I don't tell her of a seven-step process for fixing her problems. In all honesty, I don't have very good answers for her problems. All I can do is listen when she wants to talk about her hurts, cry with her when she weeps, and pray that God will grant her a few incandescent moments of joy to carry her through the years ahead.

Life includes inescapable conditions. There is nothing we mortals can do about some things. Oh, sure. Medical science will probably continue to make progress in its battles against various diseases, but death and illness will always plague us because that is the nature of being human. Life includes difficulties we don't seek and detours we didn't expect or intend. At those times, we are left almost inarticulate.

"Life is more difficult than I thought," a friend said recently. "Sometimes I don't know which way to go. Reality, for the most part, cannot simply be altered to suit our convenience or circumstances."

Another friend was born with no hands, and another has terminal cancer. A loved one dies. A relationship ends. An accident leaves a young man paralyzed from the waist down. Whether congenital or circumstantial, these facts will never be changed. The physical problems, and many of the emotional problems they entail, may never be solved.

Many large problems won't be solved in our lifetime, if they're solved at all. In spite of the extraordinary efforts of many organizations and countless committed people, the solution to world hunger still eludes us. The problem is not that we don't have sufficient resources but often how we choose to distribute them. The complexity of this situation cannot be overestimated, nor can its seriousness: about 40,000 children die each day from starvation. As much as I've encouraged you to have fun in this book, I realize there are problems in this world such as hunger that are no fun.

In his book *The Healing Choice*, Ron Lee Davis says, "I suppose we could not find any more real pulse of mankind than the pulse of pain. The Word of God throbs with the pulsation of human pain. King David long ago said, the trials of the righteous are many. Job observed that man's days are short-lived and full of turmoil. Jesus said in this world we will suffer tribulations. Paul said we should not be troubled by turmoil because we are destined for it. And Peter said we should not think it strange when we Christians endure fiery trials."

Such trials are inescapable. "In this life," writes Davis, "we will encounter hurts and trials that we will not be able to change. We are just going to have to allow them to change us. In times of trial, God often has our undivided attention. People most interested in God aren't always theologians—but people in foxholes, up to their ears in difficulties. If we are aware of God and our own limitations and powerlessness, then the question is, are we teachable? Are we attentive to the way He wants to touch us? To the insight He wants to teach us?"

However hopeless they may seem, unsolvable problems offer us a new opportunity to listen to God in brand new ways.

Cradled within the human predicament is the fact that some problems are beyond our ability to resolve, and when we find ourselves struggling with them, we are tormented by anguish, bewilderment, and even disillusionment. We must remember during those dark times what God has taught us during times of the light.

Sometimes we bring the most difficult problems upon ourselves. Sometimes we make difficult problems unsolvable by refusing to work on them while they are still solvable.

When we encounter these seemingly unsolvable problems, we need to turn to God and ask for His help with such questions as "How do I go on from here? How will I survive this pain and sorrow?" Sometimes in the context of unsolvable problems we have the opportunity to discover a new strength to our lives that is more profound than anything we've ever imagined or hoped for. In those moments we find a timeless coherence that is based on truths which do not come from us.

I waited patiently for God to help me; then he listened and heard my cry. He lifted me out of the pit of despair, out from the bog and the mire and set my feet on a hard, firm path and steadied me as I walked along. He has given me a new song to sing. . . . Now many will hear of the glorious things he did for me, and stand in awe before the Lord, and put their trust in him.

Ps. 40:1–3, LB

One of my favorite stories in the New Testament is the one of Jesus walking on the Sea of Galilee. Whereas the disciples were afraid, Peter demonstrated incredible audacity. Joining Jesus on the water, he was doing all right—until he lost his focus on Jesus and began to concentrate on "water walking." In his fearfulness, he sank.

Funny thing about Peter, rather than treading water, swimming back to the boat, or heading for the shore—that is, rather than trying to figure out or otherwise solve his problem—Peter simply looked to Jesus and uttered one of the shortest prayers you can: "Lord, help me!"

Jesus didn't say, "Sorry, Peter, that was a pretty poor prayer." Instead, Jesus reached out and caught him. To God there isn't such a thing as a poor prayer. The only ineffective prayer is the one that isn't prayed.

Peter can teach us a lot about unsolvable problems. Sometimes the best we can do is to place our focus on Jesus and cry out, "Lord, help me!"

Sometimes unanswered questions and unsolvable problems can be the real beginning of a much deeper faith experience. I believe at times like this that we are called to "chronic faith,"

incorrigible faith, and what I would call "reckless receivership."
It's at these times that we need to receive *all* that God wants to
give us. Sometimes it's more difficult to allow ourselves to be
loved by God than it is to love Him, more difficult to accept His
faith in us than our faith in Him. We *always* underestimate God's
power.

The Apostle Paul reminds us that the grief and pain from our
unsolvable problems can have a purpose, can give us an authentic
faith to share with others who are going through similar trials.
God wants to take the scars and wounds in our lives and translate
them through His grace into a means of comfort and healing in
the lives of others. Paul says that God is "the source of all mercy
and comfort. For he gives us comfort in all our trials so that we
may in turn be able to give the same sort of strong sympathy to
others in their troubles that we receive from God. Indeed, experience shows that the more we share in Christ's immeasurable
suffering the more we are able to give of his encouragement"
(2 Cor. 1:3–5, PHILLIPS).

Occasionally, our lives are too neat and tidy for God to be able
to invade our situations. As James Dittes said, "We try so hard to
be strong men and undivided and to bind the Lord, His church
and His ministry in swaddling clothes and to lay them in a stable
place. But our full and ordered house shuts Him out—just like
the inn in Bethlehem. Perhaps it is just to a divided nation, a
ruptured community, a torn family, a split self, a chaotic sense of
vocation, and an impossible church that Christ and His call comes
most profoundly."

It is in the middle of our brokenness, in our overwhelming frustration over unsolvable problems, in our despair, in our anguish, in
our doubts that Christ comes most fully. Christ is the man of our
"middle times."

> Between the exhilaration of Beginning . . .
> and the satisfaction of Concluding
> Is the Middle Time
> of Enduring . . . Changing . . . Trying . . .
> Despairing . . . Continuing . . . Becoming

Jesus Christ was the Man of God's Middle Time
Between Creation . . . and Accomplishment
Through Him God said of Creation,
"Without mistake."
And of Accomplishment
"Without Doubt."

And we in our Middle Time
of Wondering and Waiting

Hurrying and Hesitating
Regretting and Revising
We who have begun many things
and seen but few completed . . .
We who are becoming more . . . and less . . .
through the evidence of God's
Middle Time

Have a stabilizing hint
That we are not mistakes
That we are irreplaceable,
That our being is of interest,
And our doing is of purpose,
That our being and our doing
Are surrounded by AMEN.

17

Relational Problems

I know that you believe you understand what you think I said, but I'm not sure you realize that what you heard is not what I meant.

It's not the giants who defeat us, but the mosquitoes.

Gage Spindler

There are two things that will make a critical difference to your success in life: (1) getting along with people and (2) creative thinking.

It is much nicer to be in love than in an automobile accident, a tight girdle, a higher tax bracket, or a holding pattern over Atlanta. But not if the object of your love doesn't love you back.

Question: What's the difference between infatuation and love?

Answer: Infatuation is when you think that he's as sexy as Robert Redford, as smart as Stephen Hawking, as noble as Aleksandr Solhenitsyn, as funny as Robin Williams, and as athletic as Arnold Swartzenegger. Love is when you realize he's as

178

sexy as Stephen Hawking, as smart as Arnold Swartzenegger, as funny as Aleksandr Solhenitsyn, as athletic as Robin Williams, and nothing at all like Robert Redford, but you take him anyway.

LOVE IN CONTEXT

At 7 A.M., she's wide awake and ready to take on the world; I'm still comatose. I believe that if God had meant for me to see morning, he would have put it later in the day.

One thing can be said about the speed of light, it always comes too early in the morning.

Pam and I have awakened in the same bed 6,572 mornings. We've dined together more than 19,710 times. So, why is it I can only remember a handful of those moments? We've shared the birth of two sons. I remember vividly the first time when Pam told me that I was going to be a father. We were in the middle of Mission Boulevard. In the excitement, I almost got run over. I was present at the birth of our son, Zac, now fourteen. Just the other day I offered him a pair of my old shoes. He said, "Dad, I'd like to take them, but they are too small." And then when Josh was born, we waited so long at the house because Pam preferred watching television to lying around the hospital that she almost gave birth in the car on the 210 Freeway. Josh was born twenty minutes after we arrived at Arcadia Presbyterian Hospital. And now our lives revolve around CAT scores, soccer balls, algebraic equations, subjunctive clauses, and the facts of life.

It's all going so fast that I sometimes want to push the pause button between homework assignments, basketball games, pizza and a video, and book reports. Today was Josh's first day of junior high school. Tomorrow is Zac's first day of high school. Yesterday they were both in kindergarten.

Whatever happened to 1982? Whatever happened to the night when six kittens were born at midnight? When we thought it was all over, a seventh shivering and struggling kitten made its way into the world. Was it that long ago when we all shed tears of joy when we knew that "Garfield" was going to live?

Where are all those Sunday afternoons and the difficult conversations at 2 A.M.?

RELATIONSHIPS ARE MADE OF THIS

The hurts, the healings, the hopes, the broken dreams, and the chocolate ripple stuff of love have all been different from what we expected. They've been both much harder, and much more satisfying than we expected. We've had times when we thought we wouldn't make it and times we hoped would never end. Psychologists can identify various stages of relationships ranging from romance, to disillusionment, to commitment. We have tasted deeply of each of these. We've argued, and we've held our tongues. We've broken up fights between the kids, and they've interrupted ours. We've chased each other through sprinklers and banged on locked doors. We've been through chicken pox, broken toys, and broken hearts. Whatever happened to fifth grade? We've been through fixing fences, foul language, talking about Jesus, and burnt barbecue hamburgers.

It used to be "look both ways before you cross the street" and "do you have a warm hat?" Now it's "turn down the stereo" and "have you finished your algebra yet?" Who'd have ever guessed that love would be so real, so difficult, so demanding, so confusing? "Love is attractive," someone once said, "but the practice is very difficult." It's so vital and so baffling. It's a living thing. It seems to thrive in the face of all of life's hazards. And it seems to be able to endure just about anything, except neglect.

Relational problems, unlike puzzles and riddles, are "living" problems. We only solve them piece by piece, and never once and for all. Because we are all so different, conflict is inevitable. And because we are human beings, there is no such thing as an isolated, single, untangled relational problem.

When I was writing the dad's book, I decided to look up the word "father" in the dictionary. That's when I realized it comes right after "fathead" and just before "fatigue." Now I know why!

We're all looking for something so fancy and sophisticated. We all want to give impressive answers to the meaning of life. Yet the simple truth lies at our feet. Nothing in life is more important than relationships.

Many parents underestimate the significance of their roles. More moms and dads have affected—and changed—the course of history than any other single group of people or leaders. Nothing is more sacred or more difficult than being a parent.

RELATIONSHIPS APLENTY

Relationships are the essence of the quality of our lives. Whether we are single, married, divorced, widowed, or somewhere in between, our relationships and friendships form the backbone which gives meaning to our lives.

Moms, dads, brothers, sisters, friends, coworkers, teachers, students, bosses, roommates, employees, teammates—all are people with whom we have relationships. And in every case, problems are their middle name. There never has been, nor ever will be, a relationship free of problems. So how do we cope with them?

The first time I heard the word caveat in a conversation I was intrigued. So I asked "the dumb question." I didn't have any idea what it meant. I was informed that in the original Latin *caveat emptor* means "let the buyer beware." It is a warning or "caution." In a sense, to say there is a caveat means there is some risk of miscommunication or misunderstanding.

I have subsequently learned that another form of the phrase "caveat lector" means "let the reader beware," and that, too, is sometimes an appropriate warning or caution. It's a disclaimer of sorts. Well, I have a "caveat lector" for this chapter.

It is combined audacity and sheer naiveté on my part to presume that in this book I can offer a single chapter on human relationships. Volumes have been written on this subject. Since the days of Adam and Eve, human beings have been trying to gain some insight into how we can improve our relationships. And starting with Adam and Eve, we've had a tough time of it. If you're married, have children, or work, you have relational problems.

Troubled relationships are not limited to those between human beings. After they blew it in the Garden of Eden, Adam and Eve had great difficulty in their relationships with God. God's first question to man was, "Adam, why are you hiding?" And when God asked the critical question, "Have you eaten fruit from the tree I warned you about?" Adam admitted, "Yes . . . but it was the woman you gave me who brought me

some." Eve made some excuses, too. And since that day, relationships between peoples and between individuals and God have
been troubled (Gen. 3:9ff.).

Nevertheless, some of the principles we've looked at earlier in
this book about problem solving also apply to solving problems in
relationships.

Part of our problem is that we humans are so wonderfully complex. At every moment of our lives, trillions of cells are fusing into
a biochemical matrix and are bringing together all that we are. Even
for the saints of God, life doesn't seem to follow a neat, seminar-
notebook outline.

BASICS

Here are four simple ideas to consider when wrestling with
relational problems.

First, most of us spend much of our time responding or reacting
to symptoms in a relationship rather than finding out what the
problem really is so we can creatively work toward some resolution.

Second, when describing a relational problem, think of verbs
rather than nouns. Don't just say that he or she is a klutz. That
only labels the person and makes problem solving more difficult
than it should be. Instead, define the problem in verbs: he or she
is doing such and such which really bothers me.

Third, beware of either/or categories. If you're stuck in one of
these categories, then you have a pretty good sign that neither
option will work for you. We want to be "right" so much that we
lose the ability to solve the problem. A win/lose situation usually
means that both parties will eventually lose.

Fourth, each of us is 100 percent responsible for all of our
relational difficulties. This may seem like a shocking thing to say,
and I know the disbelief that this statement first produces. Nevertheless, it is true. If you have a problem then you must be part
of the solution. The first time I heard this principle I was also
shocked. A friend of mine and his wife were going through great
difficulties which eventually led to a divorce. I was spending
much time with David trying to listen and learn and be of some
help to him. Pam shocked me by saying, "David will never even

begin to solve some of his problems with Katherine until he realizes that it is 100 percent his fault."

I quickly came to his defense saying, "She's not completely innocent in this whole thing. I know David has really made some big mistakes, but she's got to have some of the responsibility, too."

My wife responded, "Yes, Katherine is also 100 percent responsible for the relationship."

Too often we think our relationships are percentages such as 50/50 or 60/40 or 70/30, but in reality the mathematics of relationships are really 100/100. Going halfway has never been God's solution for a relationship. Each of us is *totally* responsible for the relationship because the only person that you can ever change is yourself. If you want to help your spouse, or child, or friend, or whomever, then work on problems rather than symptoms. Recognize again and again that the only person you have real power to change is yourself. Nothing is a greater obstacle to being in good relationships with others than being ill at ease with yourself. When you want more passion in your life, more zest, put more into yourself and your relationship with God. If you rely solely on others to provide your life's passion, you'll usually be frustrated.

Self-love is too often confused with vanity and pride. We think it's selfish to love ourselves, when in reality it is selfish *not* to love ourselves. When we don't love ourselves we *take from others* in order to fill our own emptiness. It is important to realize that the better I feel about myself, the better I usually feel about my relationships.

All of our relationships with people begin with our relationship with God. Christ has shown Himself among us. God has made His dwelling place within us. And this is what sets us free to love each other. Unfortunately, we often expect the world or others to provide us with the kind of peace, security, and love which only comes from the kingdom of God dwelling within us.

REALIZE THE IMPORTANCE OF RELATIONSHIPS

In the Chinese language, whole words are written with a symbol. Often two completely different symbols put together have a meaning quite different than either of their two separate components. For example, the symbols for "man" and for "woman" when combined mean "good."

Likewise, when you take the symbol for "trouble" and "gathering crisis" and put them together they mean "opportunity." As the answers to life always lie in the questions, so the opportunities of life lie in our problems.

Some people have strong, loving relationships with people around them who support and enhance their lives. So, they're excited to discover more about relational situations to further enhance the relationships they already have. Others are in situations where their lines of communication may have broken down in some of the most important relationships of their lives, such as within their families. I must confess that at times I have been totally overwhelmed with relational problems. If we're honest, we probably all have.

Relationships add great richness to our lives, but they can also add great pain. Within relationships exist some of life's most complex and most painful problems.

I heard a pastor once begin a sermon by saying, "As it says in Genesis, God said, 'Let there be light' and there was light. And God said it was good. And God said, 'Let the waters under the heavens be gathered together into one place and let the dry land appear.' And it was so, and it was good. And God said, 'Let there be lights in the firmament of the heavens to separate day from night.' And it was so, and God said that it was good. And God said, 'Let the waters bring forth swarms of living creatures and let the birds fly across the earth and across the firmament of the heavens.' And God saw this and said it was good. And God said, 'Let the earth bring forth living creatures according to their kind.' And it was so, and God said it was good. And finally, God made man in His image. And he said, 'It is *not* good.'"

The pastor paused, and I sat there somewhat confused. He'd done a good job enticing me. He finally said, as it says in Gen. 2:18, "It is not good that the man should be alone; I will make him a helper fit for him" (RSV).

We were designed for relationships. We were made to be with

each other, to grow with each other, to discover each other, and to love each other. But it's not all quite as simple as that. We must forge our relationships together with effort and care all the while solving our problems for one another's best good as well as our own.

In this light, I would like to offer a few suggestions.

FIRST, DON'T BLAME

As we noted before, Carl Jung said, "The *only* person I cannot help is one who blames others." That simple statement knocked my socks off! It has about it a profound simplicity. When we blame others, we make it difficult, if not impossible, to solve our problems.

When problems inevitably invade our lives, we must resist the temptation to accuse others. We should also avoid blaming ourselves as well. Nor should we blame God.

Focus on the problem, not the person. Figure out the problem. If there have been failures, we have to confess them in ourselves *and* forgive them in others. Put the problem in perspective and get on with problem *solving*.

SECOND, YOU CAN EITHER PROTECT OR LEARN

We can respond to conflict in two ways. Jordan and Margaret Paul point out in their book, *Do I Have to Give Up Me to Be Loved by You?* that when faced with a conflict we will either try to *protect* or *learn*. Conflict does not cause problems in relationships, instead problems evolve from *how* we respond to the conflict.

We must ask ourselves if we're trying to defend and protect ourselves, or if we're trying to learn from our experiences: "Seeing conflict as opportunity rather than as a calamity puts it in a new light. You may think it sounds ridiculous (if not impossible) to face emotional pain willingly. But it does make sense. . . . When we stop blaming our partner, we assume responsibility for our own lives . . . and change becomes possible."[1] Our relational problem

---

[1] Jordan Paul and Margaret Paul, *Do I have to Give Up Me to Be Loved by You?* (Minneapolis: CompCare Publications, 1983), 10.

solving will *always* be *unsuccessful* as long as our primary interest is protective. We must commit ourselves to openness and *learning*.

When we assume responsibility for our problems we can explore relational difficulties as process rather than seek an "answer." "The Western world has been programmed very narrowly: define problems, seek solutions, set goals, make decisions, *fix* things. Fix your spouse, fix your children, fix yourself. When we see something we don't like, we judge it and want to change it rather than understand it; we look for the immediate solution rather than seek to understand how and why the problem arose."

THIRD, DEAL WITH THE REAL ISSUES!

Most problems never get solved because they are never accepted. Although hiding from problems is easier than facing them, avoidance has never solved a problem. There is no such thing as an "appropriate" time in relational problems. Deal with your problem; don't wait. The Bible says not to let the sun go down on your anger. We must recognize when we have a problem and find the first available moment to discuss it while it's still in its proper proportion. Leftover problems, like leftover meatloaf, not only grow stale but also begin to mold. The best technique I know for doing this—and for heading off some of the problems before they get too big—is to spend fifteen or twenty minutes a day talking about your feelings and current issues.

Love is a four-letter word spelled t-i-m-e. The way you show someone you care for them is to spend time with them and listen deeply to them.

LISTEN

One of the best ways to demonstrate God's love is to listen to people.

Bruce Larsen

In *Why Can't My Mate Be More Like Me?* author Len McMillan, describes the following scene from Charles Schultz's comic strip "Peanuts."

Lucy shouts at Linus, "You blockhead!"

Linus counters, "Why did you call me a dumbbell?"

"I didn't say dumbbell, I said blockhead," Lucy replies. With chin in hand, elbows resting on the top of the wall, Lucy says to herself, "That's what causes so much trouble between people today, there is no real understanding."

The word communication comes from the Latin root *communus,* meaning to have something in common. Communication breaks down most tragically as a result of our inability to listen. According to a 1981 *U.S. News & World Report* study, the single biggest reason couples split up is the "inability to talk honestly with each other, to bare their souls, and to treat each other as their best friend."

Listening, surprisingly, is the most important aspect of communication. Professor H. W. Jurgen, a West German sociologist, claims that couples chat with each other for seventy minutes a day in their first year of marriage, dropping to thirty minutes a day in their second year and then to only fifteen minutes in the fourth. His research shows that by the eighth year a husband and wife share hardly any small talk and become nearly silent with each other.

Shocking? Not really, when you consider the findings of American scientific professor Ray Birdwhitsell. His studies show that American couples talk with each other for only 27½ minutes a week. That's a daily ration of less than four minutes a day, says McMillan in his book.[2]

Communication involves much more than words. One authority said that only 7 percent of our communication involves spoken words, another 38 percent is conveyed by body language including gestures and facial expressions, and 55 percent by the tone of our voice.

Listening is the most profound way you demonstrate to others that you love them. Strangely enough, listening is perhaps the most potent way we can affect another life. Paul Tournier said, "It is impossible to overemphasize the immense need humans have to be really listened to, to be taken seriously, to be understood. No one can develop freely in this world and find the life full, without

---

[2] Len McMillan, *Why Can't My Mate Be More Like Me?* (Boise, Idaho: Pacific Press Publishing Assoc., 1986), 67.

feeling understood by at least one person. . . . Listen to all the conversations of our world, between nations as well as between couples. They are for the most part, dialogues of the deaf."

The most important thing we can do to solve a problem is to understand it. Unfortunately, we never listen "fer enuf" to understand what the problem really is, so we in turn are never able to solve it. Instead of listening, we simply take turns talking. To listen effectively, postpone your desire to react, defend, or respond. The purpose of listening is to allow both of you to understand the situation more fully. Listening attentively makes people feel special.

Ernie Larson says, "The people I work with find it extremely helpful to get firm, concrete answers from their partners to these three questions:

1. What does it mean to you to be loved?
2. What does it take for you to feel loved?
3. What are you asking of me in this regard?

He then reveals seven levels of needs that people have to have in order to be loved.

I believe that nothing makes people feel supported, cared about, accepted, and special as much as listening to them. Active listening is responsive, attentive, considerate. It means listening with your eyes as well as your ears. When someone really listens to us, it gives us the freedom to continue exploring, at deeper levels, who we are and what the problem is. Love is best demonstrated by attentive listening.

DESIGN CREATIVE QUESTIONS

We can cultivate our listening ability by designing and asking appropriate questions. For example, have your spouse, friend, roommate, or other significant "other" complete a few sentences like:

- It would mean a lot to me if you . . .
- I love you most when . . .
- I like myself most when . . .
- I feel most loved (or most hurt) when . . .
- What if we . . .
- The three biggest irritations in my life are . . .

Dennis and Barbara Rainey wrote a book (*The Questions Book*) dealing with important questions that affect marriages. Many of their questions, however, apply to any relationship—even problem relationships. For example:

- What dreams have you thrown away (or kept secret) because no one encouraged you to try it or because you feared you would fail?
- If you could do anything in the world and be certain of success, what would you do?
- In what three specific ways could we improve our everyday communication? Where are we strong in our communicating? Where do we hit snags?
- In what simple way would you most like to see me grow personally in the next twelve months?

The list of good questions is endless. All we need to ask them are loving hearts, a desire to deepen our relationships—and practice. Really good questions are those in which both people discover something about themselves.

If you can't communicate even with the help of creative questions, then get help, if you believe it's necessary. Sometimes we unintentionally build walls that are simply too big for us to climb by ourselves. If a relationship reaches a point where the walls are too high, then a minister or another professional might be of help to you.

SEVEN-STEP PROCESS

Another thing we can do is to apply an objective process to our relational problems. Earlier, in chapter 14, we talked about seven critical steps to solving problems. What we must do is:

1. *Accept ownership of the problem.* Even if you believe that the other person is at fault, if you care about the relationship, it is still your problem. Once you accept ownership of the problem you will be willing to commit your time and energies to solving it.

2. *Analyze the problem.* Take the problem apart and identify its various components. Often this means untangling numerous problems so that you can focus on them one at a time. This is a good time to ask "dumb questions," to challenge your assumptions, to keep a broad perspective, and to avoid getting emotionally hooked.

3. *Define the problem in the best terms you know.* Develop a workable definition that all parties can agree to and write it down. It is critical here to separate the symptoms from the real cause of the problem. Remember, the flip side of cynicism is idealism. If somebody is struggling with being too cynical (that's the symptom) they need to wrestle with the problem, which is their hidden idealism. In other words, you don't try to help the person become less cynical, but help him to be more realistic—that's working on the core of the problem.

Likewise, anger and apathy are expressions of frustration (frustration begets anger begets apathy). Instead of reacting to your partner's anger or apathy, listen to his or her frustration.

4. *Brainstorm.* What are all the possible solutions that could be employed at this time? Any time you can "make-it-fun" you will improve not only the quantity of ideas, but the quality as well. Take this opportunity to listen deeply to others.

Sometimes we have to take a risk and suggest outrageous ideas. If you want change, you must be willing to think sideways, backward, around corners, and upside-down. Limiting yourself to your regular patterns of thinking restricts you to seeing what you've always seen before with little chance for change or improvement in your problem solving.

5. *Select a course of action to which everybody involved can commit.* It is important to be able to articulate clearly why you believe this is the best selection. If you know why this is the best plan, you will be much less likely to abandon it when the way becomes difficult.

6. *Implement.* You've planned your work, now work your plan. Work lovingly. There is great joy in a well-built relationship. Remember to tap the resources of the Master. To do this, bathe your work in prayer.

7. *Evaluate.* This is another chance to learn from your problem, even if you weren't successful in solving it. What you learn and how you learn will allow you to move into deeper levels of mutual understanding and appreciation.

Relational problems are process oriented. We will always be in process, but I hope that some of these techniques will enable you to gain greater definition of your problem and to find healthy, loving solutions.

In the heat of conflict, it is easy to forget the goals of your relationship. Wanting to be right is easier than wanting to be understanding. These principles of relational problem solving won't help you build your defenses, but they will help you to attack the problem and *learn* rather than attack the person and lose.

You cannot afford to neglect the incredible power of love. Remember that God is love and that he who dwells in love, dwells in God and God in him. This love makes us fearless, and where there is no fear there is true understanding. The power of God's love will never be contained nor understood. It is available to all and can literally produce miracles in relationships. Love is by far the most important of all. It casts out fear. It covers a multitude of sins. Love is absolutely invincible. "There is no difficulty that enough love will not conquer, no disease that enough love cannot heal, no door that enough love will not open, no gulf that enough love will not bridge, no wall that enough love will not throw down, no sin that enough love will not redeem.

"It makes no difference how deep the trouble, how hopeless the outlook, how muddled the tangle, how great the mistake; sufficient love will dissolve it all."[3] I believe that when we put God, who is love, in the center of our relationships He can transform them. He empowers us to influence each other's lives.

I love you,
Not only for what you are,
But for what I am
When I am with you.

I love you,
Not only for what
You have made of yourself
But for what
You are making of me.

I love you,
For the part of me
That you bring out;
I love you
For putting your hand
Into my heaped-up heart
And passing over
All the foolish, weak things
That you can't help
Dimly seeing there,
And for drawing out
Into the light
All the beautiful belongings
That no one else had looked
Quite far enough to find. . . .

You have done it
Without a touch
Without a word
Without a sign,
You have done it
By being yourself.

---

[3] I've paraphrased this from a poem by Emmet Fox.

18

Gonzo Christianity: The Ultimate Purpose of Problem Solving

What is needed . . . is a reckless abandonment to the Lord Jesus Christ—reckless and uncalculating abandonment with no reserve anywhere about it; not sad. You cannot be sad if you are abandoned absolutely.

Oswald Chambers

Unless life is lived for others, it is not worthwhile.

Mother Teresa

Love will always find a way to be practical.

Joe White

The Bible certainly does not ignore problems. In fact, the people of the Bible often had more problems because of their faith. The more closely we desire to follow Christ, the more problems we will have.

In the beginning of this book I used the quotation, "To have faith means to have problems." That quote means that the greater compassion we have for the world and the more we genuinely seek to be an authentic servant-leader in Christ, the more we will seek out and solve problems in order to set people free.

In other words, God's love sets us free *from* the many struggles we all wrestle with in order to allow us to be fully free *to* love others. And love will always find a way to be practical. To love often means to solve problems. Whether teaching someone to read or helping them find employment, love's problems may be as simple as mowing someone's lawn or as complicated as trying to find ways to solve world hunger.

We are called to be joyful, competent, compassionate servanthood in the world. This is difficult but not impossible. It is challenging but not beyond what God can and wants to do in our lives.

This is serious business, but it does not necessarily have to be somber. I met a woman recently who said that she had the unique privilege of spending some time with Mother Teresa. She and her husband spent much of the afternoon with this wonderful saint. Her husband has a delightful sense of humor, and Mother Teresa is known for her contagious joy. As they were getting ready to leave, the man couldn't resist asking, "Mother Teresa, what do you want to be when you grow up?" She smiled and said, "Well, I always wanted to be a stewardess."

We assume that all the folks in the Bible, and especially Jesus' disciples, were somehow superbly qualified for the job of servanthood. Not too long ago someone gave me a copy of a fictional letter to Jesus from the Jordan Management Consultants, which I think pretty well puts it all into perspective:

To: Jesus, Son of Joseph
Woodcrafter's Carpenter Shop
Nazareth 25922

From: Jordan Management Consultants

Dear Sir:
    Thank you for submitting the resumes of the twelve men you have picked for managerial positions in your new organization. All of them have now taken our battery of tests; and we have not only run the results through our computer, but also arranged personal interviews for each of them with our psychologist and vocational aptitude consultant.
    The profiles of all tests are included, and you will want to study each of them carefully.

As part of our service, we make some general comments for your guidance, much as an auditor will include some general statements. This is given as a result of staff consultation, and comes without any additional fee.

It is the staff opinion that most of your nominees are lacking in background, education and vocational aptitude for the type of enterprise you are undertaking. They do not have the team concept. We would recommend that you continue your search for persons of experience in managerial ability and proven capability.

Simon Peter is emotionally unstable and given to fits of temper. Andrew has absolutely no qualities of leadership. The two brothers, James and John, the sons of Zebedee, place personal interest above company loyalty. Thomas demonstrates a questioning attitude that would tend to undermine morale. We feel that it is our duty to tell you that Matthew has been blacklisted by the Greater Jerusalem Better Business Bureau; James, the son of Alphaeus, and Thaddaeus definitely have radical leanings, and they both registered a high score on the manic-depressive scale.

One of the candidates, however, shows great potential. He is a man of ability and resourcefulness, meets people well, has a keen business mind, and has contacts in high places. He is highly motivated, ambitious, and responsible. We recommend Judas Iscariot as your controller and right-hand man. All of the other profiles are self-explanatory.

We wish you every success in your new venture.

Sincerely yours,
Jordan Management Consultants

Keeping this letter in mind, consider the following parable that I heard not too long ago:

Jesus ascended into heaven where He was met by one of the archangels. The archangel was obviously excited to hear about all His experiences on earth, and so he bombarded Jesus with all kinds of questions.

He finally asked, "Jesus, what's your plan for redeeming the world?"

Jesus responded, "I've found these guys—pretty ordinary sorts—and I left it in their hands."

The archangel was quite taken aback and finally said, "Well, what's your alternate plan?"

Jesus replied, "I don't have any."

I'm still amazed and amused when I look around—or even worse, when I look into the mirror—at God's plan. What an incredible risk! It would be obviously impossible if God didn't also send His Holy Spirit to live this plan in us and through us.

It is upon this radical proposition that our faith is based. God's methods, Howard Hendricks says, invariably involves men and women. "But what kind of a man does God choose to use?" God's choice of material is diametrically opposed to man's. Man chooses an individual on the basis of what he is while God chooses an individual on the basis of what he is to become.

> It is not a question of our equipment, but of our poverty; not what we bring with us, but what He puts in us. . . . Being abandoned to God is of more value than personal holiness. Personal holiness focuses our eyes on our own whiteness; when we are abandoned to God, He works through us all the time.
>
> Oswald Chambers

And yet I'm amazed how so many of us have become simply spectators to this process. Too many of us are still passive observers of the greatest event that mankind has ever known. What on earth could be possibly more important than knowing God personally? If the claims of Christianity are true, then we've got something to celebrate!

Christianity began as a great adventure. In those early days when Christ was presenting an entirely new way of living to those around him, discipleship was an incredible challenge to one's faith. Following Jesus Christ demanded everything. Who would have ever imagined that such a vision would ever finally become, in the eyes of many, a formal and finished system to be passively received?

Tragically some Christians are more committed to petty piety than risking following the living unpredictable Jesus Christ. Some still prefer a religion filled with soft light through stained glass windows and quiet organ music, safe and undemanding rules, and a few emotional quivers. Chad Walsh once said, "I suspect that the enemy has called off his attempt to convert these people to agnosticism. After all," he says, "if a man travels far enough away from real Christianity, he is liable to see it in perspective and decide it's really true. It is much safer from Satan's point of view to vaccinate a man with a mild case of Christianity so as to protect him from the real disease." Ouch!

The term "Gonzo Christianity" comes from a story I heard about journalist Hunter Thompson who was thinking deeply about the process of journalism. He said, "Most writers tend to sit on the sidelines away from the action, detached from any sort of involvement and write as a mere spectator or observer, as to what is going on." He recommended what he called Gonzo Journalism where the journalist would jump into the middle of the fray, into the heart of the action, and, amidst all the difficulties, pains, and joys, write from the view of a participant rather than that of a spectator.

Likewise, all too many of us are passive observers of the world's deep despair, and we are called to become participants not only in that pain but in the divine story revealed in Scripture.

Some people will utilize these problem-solving skills and attitudes only to solve their own problems. To do so would be to miss not only the central purpose of this book but also the incredible joy to which God calls us. Perhaps the greatest joy in life is that of giving our lives away. When we do so, we find out what life's all about. Gonzo Christianity involves taking these problem-solving techniques, combining them with the mind of Christ, and jumping into the needs of the world through the power of the Holy Spirit. It also involves becoming one of God's instruments in solving some of the problems that our world struggles with daily.

Gonzo Christianity demands "reckless receivership" before it can demand "reckless servanthood." The key is to let God use you in a way that He has planned. "Let" is an incredibly potent word, a word of tremendous faith with volumes of meaning poured into it. It assumes the total, unconditional, unbelievable love and good will of the Father. It assumes that heaven is crammed with the good gifts that the Father wants to give His children. "Let" means saying, "Father, I give You permission to do so and so for us down here on earth." It is saying, "I invite You to do Your great work in even me."

THE JOURNEY CONTINUES

It might be of help to share something of my own journey. Having lived in chronic pain for almost fifteen years as a result of a near-fatal accident, I have become so exhausted in my attempt to serve God that I hardly know which end is up. Recently He got my full attention and said, "Stop, slow down. Be still and know that I AM God." We must listen before we can act. In fact the root of the word "obedience" is *obadare*, which means "to listen."

Our life of action must come from our commitment to stillness. Gonzo contemplation must precede Gonzo activity in the world. Perhaps the greatest example of this that I know is that of Mother Teresa. She won a Nobel Peace Prize for her incredible work in Calcutta. It is important to note that Mother Teresa is first of all a contemplative. She is first of all committed to a life of prayer. Her action in the world comes from her reckless receivership from God, from her *direct* relationship with God.

Gonzo receivership means participating in the life of Christ *directly* rather than just observing as a spectator. It must be firsthand. Our prayer life is where we make the deep connection to the living Christ. As we listen, He directs.

In the past few months I have made some radical changes in my life. For the past eighteen years I have been directing the wilderness ministry of Summit Expedition. It has been exciting and worthwhile, but the work has been so demanding, along with my constant pain, that it has left me absolutely wilted. I feel strongly that God is encouraging me now to let go, to spend more time with Him. Summit Expedition's ministry will continue under a new name, Summit Adventures. It will be the same vision, the same staff, the same goals, the same process—but it will have a new name because it will be their vision. My job was to bring it to this point and then let it go. I will continue to be involved, but I will no longer play a central role.

I hope I will go all the way back to the beginning, where I will again work *directly* with people on courses and participate again fully in what the living Christ has to teach us. I know I will especially continue to be involved in our *Go-For-It* program with the handicapped.

It is interesting to note that although our courses are incredibly adventurous, perhaps the greatest change in individual lives comes during what we call "solo"—a time where the participant is alone with God. Many people say, "No wonder lives are changed so dramatically given all the adventurous things you do." I remind them that lives are changed most when they sit still in the presence of God—that is the Great Adventure.

My health has diminished seriously over the past several years. God is telling me to take some time for renewal. This will be a season of absolute, radical dependence upon Him. I am looking forward to it. Contemplation and prayer must always precede action. A friend of mine reminded me that Moses said in essence in Exod. 33:14-15: "If you ain't going with me God, I ain't moving." That's important for all of us to remember. We must receive before we can give.

Once we open up the door, God can go to work. That God should wait for our permission to bestow such wonderful gifts on us requires an almost preposterous humility on God's part. It also presumes a preposterous kind of openness on our part.

If some of us feel unqualified, it's because we are. We are absolutely unqualified to do God's work. Only He can do it within us.

Gonzo Christianity simply invites us to be God's people— whoever we are, wherever we are. None of us can throw a stone in any direction from where we are right now and not find someone in more need than we are.

ONE AT A TIME

The late author Catherine Marshall told the following story about a couple named Mary and Harold Brinig who found the true basis of happiness some years ago.

This couple moved to Chicago where they had no friends, and they soon became irritable and unhappy with each other.

While seeking help from the Bible, they saw these words of Jesus: "You did not choose me, but I chose you and appointed you that you should go and bear fruit and that your fruit should abide" (John 15:16, RSV). Somehow that passage became like light penetrating their darkness. They realized that much of their unhappiness was caused by self-centeredness. They wondered if Jesus was choosing them for some kind of unknown service. They also wondered what type of service they could possibly perform in such a big city as Chicago.

The first person they encountered after this discovery was the waitress who served them in a nearby restaurant. She apologized for giving such slow service and said she was new in the city and miserable. They invited her to visit them in their apartment after work.

A neighbor who was a widower became the second person they befriended. Soon a dozen people were meeting together once a week for conversation and prayer.

Out of these meetings grew a project called "Adventures in Friendship." Soon scores of people were involved in visiting the lonely and the shut-ins throughout the whole area.

Mary and Harold became so absorbed in the needs of others that they soon forgot their troubles and their lives became richer and fuller. Their lives were filled with joy.[1]

About twenty years ago, Bruce Larson wrote a brilliant and challenging book entitled *Dare to Live Now* in which he said, "any kind of personal relationship with Christ which does not involve us with a suffering world for which Christ died is certainly an affront to the very Lord who is in His world suffering with all His people.

"The world is divided into three classes: the few who make things happen, the many who watch things happen, and the overwhelming majority who have no notion what happens."

Christianity is not like a football game where only eleven can play at a time while the rest of us watch. Too many of us are on the sidelines. Too many of us are on the shelf indefinitely preparing to get involved. Many of us claim that we would be involved if only there were more opportunities.

Oswald Chambers hit the nail on the head when he said, "Looking for opportunities to serve God is an impertinence;

---

[1] Catherine Marshall, *A Closer Walk* (Fleming H. Revell, 1986), 74–76.

every time and all the time is our opportunity to serve God. God does not expect us to work for Him but with Him."

As we've noted before, ours is a society that is more concerned with image, than substance. We are more concerned with style than genuine content. Gonzo Christianity challenges us to break through the subtle style-over-substance force in our culture and let loose the living God in our lives.

"Someday," says Teilhard de Chardin, "after mastering the winds, the waves, the tides, and gravity, we shall harness for God the energies of love and then, for the second time in the history of the world, man will have discovered fire."

This kind of love must always find a way to be practical. Paul declares to the Colossians that his primary goal in life is to make the gospel real. He says the central mystery of the gospel is "Christ in you, the hope of Glory" (Col. 1:27, RSV). This is good news. In fact, this is astonishing news: Christ in you. Christ is not merely for us; He is in us. And we are complete in Him.

Richard Halverson said, "When Christ was on earth, he was limited by time and space. In His body, He couldn't be two places at once. Think how wonderful it would be to multiply the presence of Christ by a million, or 10 million, or 100 million. That's the substance of this mystery, which is precisely the point of Pentecost. Wherever Christians are present, Christ is present—not only with them, but in them.

Halverson further poses the following challenge in his article, "Christ and You—The Hope of Glory": "Where are you going tomorrow morning? Christ is there in your body. Christ is there as much as He is in His own body. He is literally present wherever you are tomorrow morning and Tuesday, and Wednesday, and Thursday. For years many of us have thought that the only time we do anything for Christ is when we do something consciously spiritual. It is as though we thought one could turn Christ on and off in the body. He said, 'You *are* the salt of the earth.' He didn't say you may be or that you ought to be. He said you are the salt of the earth. He said you *are* the light of the world. We don't turn the light on. He does. All He asks for is a life that is willing and open."

Gonzo Christianity is the willingness to be involved, the willingness to be open to God's leadership. It is the willingness to be used by God for His purposes here and now and usually in such simple ways. As Mother Teresa says, "We can do no great things; only small things with great love."

Compassion is not necessarily quantitative. Several years ago World Vision developed a wonderful poster which said in big bold letters across the top, "How Do You Feed a Hungry World?" In the bottom right-hand corner was a tiny picture of a child and these words in small type: "One at a Time."

In Gonzo fashion, set out to conquer the world by conquering your problems one at a time with Christ at your side. He will help you as you take the principles of this book and the principles of the Bible and incarnate them into your life.

Go with peace and assurance that there is no problem you and Christ cannot handle together.

Appendix

Pocket Principles:
A Summary of Practical Tools for Problem Solving

This might be what you would call a "Problem Solver's Survival Kit." You have read and absorbed an immense amount of content. My greatest concern at this point is that you actually use it. Therefore, I've provided a final review of sorts with last minute suggestions of a very practical nature for you to employ. You might want to tear these pages out of the book, or make a dozen copies of this section and put it around your workplaces and on your refrigerator door at home so that it will provide a system of recall and application for you.

Remember, there are only two responses to communication—you can either "protect" or "learn." I trust, by now, that your primary attitude is the latter and that you will approach problems with an open and eager attitude.

ATTITUDE: UNTIL FURTHER NOTICE
CELEBRATE EVERYTHING

Problems are normal. It is in this whole process of meeting and solving problems that life has meaning. They are the cutting edge of our growth. Don't panic . . . relax . . . detach yourself a bit

. . . and begin to employ some of the key principles and processes described in this book.

Remember that the primary core of all problem solving is your attitude. Go after Moby Dick with a harpoon and tartar sauce. Avoiding problems only amplifies them. Jesus is the divine *Yes* (2 Cor. 1:19). Don't forget that! He is available to assist you in your attitude and perspective. Remember also that each of these problems will stretch, challenge, deepen your walk with Him. If we lack any wisdom (or if our attitude or perspective is distorted), we simply need to ask Him, and He has promised to provide graciously and liberally (James 1:5).

WRITE IT DOWN

Again, don't be surprised if you're having problems. That's what life's all about. Problems are normal. They're the only way we can grow. To have faith means to have problems—and there is no such thing as a problem without a gift in it. To live is to have problems—lots of them, so jump in with all four feet. Attitude is the key. If you want to feel enthusiastic, act enthusiastic. God trusts you enough to allow you to have this problem. We in turn must trust Him enough to seek a solution. If you can't change the problem, then let the problem change you. Give the problem your full attention. See it as a challenge or an opportunity rather than a threat or an obstacle. Be optimistic in your approach. Consider yourself a creative thinker. Begin to organize your approach. Get a pad and a pencil, or a notebook, and write down what you think the problem is and what some of your resources are.

RESOURCES

List all your resources. *Where* has this problem been dealt with before? *Who* do you know that might have some input on this problem or could help you define it more carefully? Who would be willing just to listen? Write down the names of people, places, and things that could be used as your resources. Focus on the positive. Stay enthusiastic and confident. Your faith controls your imagination and your emotions. Beware of these "killer phrases":

It's too big for me.
The timing's not right.
I'm not ready for this.
Let's wait and see.
Here we go again.
Why are *my* problems worse than everyone else's?

You might even in your notebook try "mind mapping," such as below. Some people find this to be an effective way of organizing their thoughts. State the problem in simple terms in the middle of the chart. List the main components of it on lines emanating from the central problem. As you break down each component, add lines branching off and label them accordingly. Continue branching off with new ideas. By branching you can discover other problems hiding behind your central problem. Place these at the center of a new cluster, and continue to branch off.

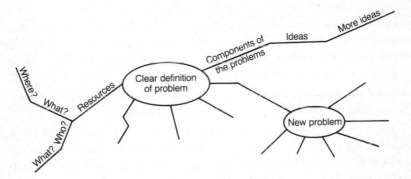

Set aside some time to deal with this problem, perhaps at your peak period, your highest energy period during the day. Remember you are in charge.

PRINCIPLES: HOW TO KEEP THE ELEPHANTS
OFF YOUR AIRHOSE

1. *Challenge your assumptions.* What kind of assumptions are you making? Write them down or discuss them with a friend. Try to state the problem from as many different angles as possible and recognize the potential sand traps of assumptions. Especially be

aware of assumptions such as "I'm not creative" or "I'm not a good problem solver."

2. *Keep a broad perspective.* How is your perspective on the problem? Is it big enough? Could it be increased? Are you making mole hills into mountains? Or mountains into mole hills? Open some windows on some of the countless possibilities to your current situation. Beware of "a hardening of the categories." The truth is that you don't let the darkness out, but you let the light in. Have you truly surrendered this to Him? Have you really let go?

3. *Don't get "hooked."* Is there any part of the problem that has "hooked" you emotionally? If so, get a friend and talk about it. Get it off your chest. Talk about it until you can detach yourself enough that you can really be objective about the problem.

4. *Simple is better.* Is there some simple answer that you're possibly overlooking? Look for the simplest pattern first. Try to discover the obvious. Write it down. Eliminate everything that is unnecessary, everything that is not focused on the core of the problem. (This includes eliminating excess emotions that are not a necessary part of the problem.) Who can you phone that might have a tremendous insight into this problem for you? Have you read those Scripture passages that are appropriate to what you are dealing with now? Don't overlook the obvious.

5. *Look for the second right answer.* Have you fallen in love with one of your solutions to such an extent that you're blinded to other opportunities? Look for a second solution, a second right answer. In fact, look for the "elegant" answer. Don't be satisfied with just any solution to this problem.

6. *Ask dumb questions.* Become childlike. Ask naive questions, even dumb questions. Ask lots and lots of questions. Gather as much information as you possibly can. Write down in your notebook a series of questions that will help you focus on this problem and create possible resources for its solution.

7. *Scratch where it itches.* What really is the problem? Don't kid yourself with vague ideas. Force yourself to reduce your ideas into specific propositions and objectives, thus firming up what you are trying to solve. Again, eliminate the extraneous. Use the principle

of reversal. Look at your problem from the other direction—look at it from the top, the bottom, the right, the left, the inside, and the outside. Try to explain it as precisely as possible to someone else and then listen to yourself talk. Write the problem down. Define it, redefine it, and then redefine it again. A problem well stated is a problem half solved.

8. *Unlock your creativity.* Turn loose your God-given gift of creativity. You are the only expert on your own life. Release some of the innate genius within you. Thinking horizontally as well as vertically. Toss the problem back and forth. Ask more questions. Write down ideas and then play them. Here again is another place to use "clustering" or "mind mapping."

9. *Make it fun.* There's no more important time to keep your sense of humor alive than when you are trying to tackle a difficult problem. If you can, laugh at the problem. If you can't, laugh at yourself. Remember "a cheerful heart is a good medicine" (Prov. 17:22, RSV). If you can't have fun with problem solving, if you are taking yourself much too seriously, put the problem aside and go see a funny movie. Or read a *Reader's Digest* joke section. Go back and solve a couple of these crazy puzzles. You are most effective when you are doing something you enjoy. If there's any way you can celebrate any facet of this problem, do it.

10. *Hang in there.* Have you gone "fer enuf"? Are you giving up too soon? If you are tempted to give up perhaps you need to put the problem on a back burner and let it "incubate." Write it down somewhere, file it for a period of time, then come back to it. This will increase your creativity and your ability to persevere. Remember that some problems take time. If you can, put your problem in an eternal perspective. Remember number ten!

A Seven-step Process

Remember the seven steps.

1. *Recognize and accept that it is a problem.* Have you really accepted it? In the sense that you are willing to engage it fully and give it all your attention. This is, and always will be, the beginning point of problem solving. It's your problem. Don't blame or project it on others. Own it!

2. *Analyze the problem.* Discover what it looks like. Get to know the ins and outs of it. Simplify it. Take it apart. Take a close look at each piece. Solve the smaller pieces first. Get some kind of handle on it.

3. *Define the problem.* This is undoubtedly the most important step in problem solving. What is the main issue? Clarify your major goal or goals in solving the problem. Where do you want to be when this problem is solved? What will it look like? Don't look for solutions yet. Separate symptoms from problems. Get to the heart of the matter.

4. *Brainstorm.* Perhaps the most unused gift in the Kingdom of God is each other. Brainstorm with some friends. The wilder the ideas, the better. Again, write them down. Search out all the ways possible of exploring this problem. Seek as many alternatives as you can. Quantity at this point is more important than quality. Seek and ye shall find.

5. *Select.* Take a chance. Choose which one you think is the best possible way of solving the problem at this time and then . . . go for it!

6. *Implement.* Put it into action. Go to work. Give it your best shot. This is where the hard work begins. You've got to go from theory to reality. Do it, and do it now!

7. *Evaluate.* Did it work? Or didn't it? Was it only partially effective? If so, if your problem's not solved to your satisfaction, then go back and go through the process again. Problem solving is a continual process, so celebrate each part.

Here's a pop quiz, just to see how your problem solving has improved since you've read this book:

1. Where was Paul going on the road to Damascus?
2. Do they have a fourth of July in England?
3. Some months have thirty days, some have thirty-one. How many have twenty-eight days?
4. Why can't a man living in Winston-Salem, North Carolina, be buried west of the Mississippi River?
5. A farmer had seventeen sheep. All but nine died. How many does he have left?

6. Take two apples from three apples and what do you have?
7. If a rooster laid an egg on the top of a hill, which side would the egg roll down?
8. How many birthdays does an average man have?
9. An archaeologist claimed he found some coins in Italy dated 46 B.C. Is he reliable?
10. How many three-cent stamps are there in a dozen?

You'll find the answers at the end of this appendix.

REALITY—WHAT A CONCEPT!

Remember that the most important and most difficult problems are relational ones. Some of them are unsolvable. That means again that if you can't change them, then let them change you.

At times you have to take your eyes off yourself and focus them on Christ and His great purposes for the world. When your joy dissipates, when life seems to overwhelm you, look for somebody who is worse off than you are, then try to help them. Your joy will amazingly return to you in new dimensions. Joy is doubled when it's divided between us. The most satisfying thing that we can ever do in life is to help another person. Find a cause, a purpose, or a person that you can help support. Our dignity grows in direct proportion to how much we are doing for others. Do at least one small thing to change the world, even if it's just in an ever-so-subtle way. Let your life make a difference.

ANSWERS TO POP QUIZ

1. Damascus. 2. Of course. 3. All twelve do. 4. It's illegal to bury live people. 5. Nine. 6. Two apples 7. Roosters don't lay eggs. 8. One. 9. No. 10. Twelve.

References

Adams, James L. *Conceptual Blockbusting.* 2d ed. New York: W. W. Norton & Co., 1980.

Berry, Carmen Renee. *When Helping You Is Hurting Me.* New York: Harper & Row, 1988.

Bowman, Bruce. *Ideas: How to Get Them.* Saratoga, Calif.: R & E Publishers, 1985.

Bransford, John D., and Barry S. Stein. *The Ideal Problem Solver: A Guide to Improving Thinking, Learning, and Creativity.* New York: W. H. Freeman and Co., 1984.

Buechner, Frederick. *Whistling in the Dark.* New York: Harper & Row, 1988.

Campbell, David. *Take the Road to Creativity and Get off Your Dead End.* Valencia, Calif.: Argus Communications, 1985.

Cheney, Lois. *God Is No Fool.* Nashville: Abingdon, 1969.

Davis, Ron Lee. *Gold in the Making.* Nashville: Thomas Nelson Publishers, 1984.

——. *The Healing Choice.* Waco, Tex.: Word Books, 1986.

De Bono, Edward. *New Think.* New York: Avon Books, 1971.

Fixx, James. *Games for the Superintelligent.* Garden City, N.Y.: Doubleday & Co., 1972.

————. *More Games for the Superintelligent*. Garden City, N.Y.: Doubleday & Co., 1976.

Gordon, Thomas, and Judith Sands. *P.E.T. in Action*. New York: Bantam Books, 1978.

Haggai, John Edmund. *How to Win over Worry*. Rev. ed. Harvest House, 1987.

Hanks, Kurt, et al. *Design Yourself!* Los Altos, Calif.: William Kaufmann, 1977.

Henricks, Howard G. *Taking a Stand/What God Can Do through Ordinary You!* Portland, Oreg.: Multnomah Press, 1972.

Hover, Herman. *How Many Three Cent Stamps in a Dozen?* Los Angeles: Price Stern Sloan, 1976.

Kimmel, Tim. *Little House on the Freeway: Help for the Hurried Home*. Portland, Oreg.: Multnomah Press, 1987.

Koberg, Don, and Jim Bagnall. *Universal Traveler: A Soft-Systems Guide to Creativity, Problem-Solving, and the Process of Reaching Goals*. Rev. ed. Los Altos, Calif.: William Kaufmann, 1981.

Larsen, Earnie. *Stage II Relationships*. New York: Harper & Row, 1987.

Larson, Bruce. *Dare to Live Now*. Grand Rapids, Mich.: Zondervan Publishing House, 1965.

Lockerbie, D. Bruce. *The Timeless Moment*. Santa Barbara, Calif.: Cornerstone Books, 1980.

Longley-Cook, L. H. *Fun for Puzzle People*. New York: Fawcett Books, 1977.

————. *More Puzzle Fun*. New York: Fawcett Books, 1979.

Lucado, Max. *God Came Near*. Portland, Oreg.: Multnomah Press, 1987.

Marshall, Catherine. *A Closer Walk*. Old Tappan, N.J.: Fleming H. Revell and Co., 1985.

McMillan, Len D. *Why Can't My Mate Be More Like Me?* Boise, Idaho: Pacific Press Publishing Assoc., 1986.

Meberg, Marilyn. *Choosing the Amusing: What Difference Does It Make*. Portland, Oreg.: Multnomah Press, 1986.

O'Connor, Elizabeth. *Eighth Day of Creation*. Waco, Tex.: Word Books, 1971.

Ogilvie, Lloyd J. *If God Cares, Why Do I Still Have Problems?* Waco, Tex.: Word Books, 1985.

Osborn, Alex F. *Applied Imagination.* New York: Charles Scribner's Sons, 1953.

Peters, Tom. *Thriving on Chaos: A Revolutionary Agenda for Today's Manager.* New York: Alfred A. Knopf, 1987.

Prince, George M. *The Practice of Creativity: A Manual for Dynamic Group Problem Solving.* New York: Collier Books, 1972.

Raudsepp, Eugene, and George P. Hough, Jr. *Creative Growth Games.* San Diego, Calif.: Harvest Books, 1977.

Rayburn, Jim, III. *Dance, Children, Dance.* Wheaton, Ill.: Tyndale House Publishers, 1984.

Roberts, Stan, and Larry Sloan. *The World's Worst Riddles.* Los Angeles: Price Stern Sloan, 1974.

Rodgers, Buck. *The IBM Way: Insights into the World's Most Successful Marketing Organization.* New York: Harper & Row, 1987.

Sheldon, Charles M. *In His Steps.* Westwood, N.J.: Barbour and Co., 1897.

Sullivan, Patrick B. *Bets You Can't Lose.* Los Angeles: Price Stern Sloan, 1979.

————. *More Bets You Can't Lose.* Los Angeles: Price Stern Sloan, 1983.

Von Oech, Roger. *A Kick in the Seat of the Pants.* New York: Harper & Row , 1986.

————. *A Whack on the Side of the Head: How to Unlock Your Mind for Innovation.* New York: Warner Books, 1983.

Wakefield, Norman. *Solving Problems Before They Become Conflicts.* Grand Rapids, Mich.: Zondervan Publishing House, 1987.

Welter, Paul. *Learning from Children.* Wheaton, Ill.: Tyndale House, 1984.

Williams, Linda V. *Teaching for the Two-Sided Mind: A Guide to Right Brain-Left Brain Education.* New York: Simon & Schuster, 1983.

Woods, Ralph. *Mind Teasers.* Los Angeles: Price Stern Sloan, 1982.

————. *More Mind Teasers.* Los Angeles: Price Stern Sloan, 1986.

For all that has been—Thanks.
To all that shall be—YES!
Dag Hammarskjold

Tim Hansel is a nationally known speaker and seminar leader. For more information about problem-solving seminars, speaking engagements, books, or films, write or phone:

Tim Hansel
P.O. Box 521
San Dimas, Calif. 91773
(818) 915-3331

For Life-Changing Wilderness Adventures please contact:

Dave Kelley, Director
Summit Adventures
P.O. Box 498
Bass Lake, CA 93604
(209) 642-3899
(209) 642-3890